*... the grand piano*
*came by camel*

Arthur C. Mace, the neglected Egyptologist

CHRISTOPHER C. LEE

*Arthur Mace at work in the laboratory during the excavation of the tomb of Tutankhamun.*

# ... the grand piano came by camel

## Arthur C. Mace, the neglected Egyptologist

### CHRISTOPHER C. LEE

MAINSTREAM
PUBLISHING
EDINBURGH AND LONDON

First published in Great Britain in 1992 by
MAINSTREAM PUBLISHING COMPANY (EDINBURGH) LTD
7 Albany Street
Edinburgh EH1 3UG


ISBN 1 85158 434 X (cloth)

A catalogue record for this book is available from the British Library


Designed by Maxine Scott
Typeset in Times
Bureau output by Davidson van Breugel, Glasgow G3 7SL
Printed in Great Britain by Martin's of Berwick Ltd

---

FOR MY MOTHER

and for

JACQUELINE, MATTHEW AND JONATHAN

---

Though thou departest, thou comest again; though thou sleepest,
thou wakest again; though thou diest, thou livest again.
Stand up, that thou mayest see what thy son has done for thee ...

From the Pyramid Texts quoted by A. C. Mace in *Egyptian Literature*
(1928).

If thou art a man of position, gain respect by wisdom, and by
quietness of speech.

From the proverbs of a wise man named Ptahhotep quoted by A. C. Mace
in *Egyptian Literature* (1928).

# Acknowledgements

There can be few more satisfying sights than that of one's own name on the front cover of a book. At the same time it also produces an intense feeling of embarrassment in the knowledge that the production of a book owes a great deal directly or indirectly to a large number of people other than the author.

This book about the life and work of Arthur C. Mace would never have seen the light of day had it not been for the determination of my friend and colleague Jim Erskine, Design and Exhibitions Officer for Renfrew District Council. Jim has the enviable capacity to see light at the end of the tunnel when others cannot even see the tunnel. To him I offer my grateful thanks. I also owe a particular debt to Vivian Kerr for her support and her invaluable knowledge of the world of books and publishing. In addition I have been fortunate to have as a colleague and collaborator the creative skills of a talented young designer, Maxine Scott. As someone who has been blissfully ignorant of developments like the word processor I rely heavily on the administrative and secretarial capabilities of others. Fortunately, in this respect I have had the practical assistance of Janette Carmichael and Mary Clark. Mary has shouldered most of the burden of typing, always retaining her sense of humour and always managing to calm the anxious writer. I would like to thank David Roberts for stepping in at the last minute to undertake the preparation of the index.

One of the great rewards of researching this book has been the development of a friendship with Arthur's daughter, Mrs. Margaret Orr. Our many hours of conversation have been for me a delightful and enriching experience and for this, and for permitting me to have access to her father's papers, I am deeply grateful. Margaret's children Alison, Tessa and David have also been unstinting in their support and practical assistance. Another valued friendship which has grown out of this research has been that with Marsha Hill, of the Department of Egyptian Art at the Metropolitan Museum, New York. I have benefited from her guidance and wisdom as well as her knowledge of Mace and the Metropolitan's Egyptian expeditions. Advice in matters Egyptological has come from a number of other people and I particularly want to thank Harry James, Peggy Drower, Barbara Adams and Nicholas Reeves. They have all with good nature and a sense of humour put up with the questions that I, in my ignorance of Egypt and Egyptology, have asked. Mrs. Drower in particular made many useful suggestions as well as painstakingly checking the text.

The staff and children of Lochwinnoch Primary School have played a central role in the uncovering of the story of Arthur Mace, indeed without them this book would not have appeared. I also wish to thank my colleagues in Paisley Museum and at Lochwinnoch for their support, in particular, Betty Whyte, Jem Kilburn and Stan Dundas, who held the fort while I wrote.

I would also like to acknowledge the assistance of the following: Dieter and Dorothea Arnold; Mrs. R. Berwold; Dr. M. L. Bierbrier; The Boston Museum of Fine Arts; Mr. W. V. Davis; The Egypt Exploration Society; Lorraine Fannin; Irene Freeman; Jim Hermit; Mr. & Mrs. A. Lloyd; Miss S. Lloyd; David C. Butters; Phoebe A. Hearst Museum of Anthropology, University of California at Berkeley; Dr. J. Malek; Robert S. Merrillees; Phillip K. Newell, Bishop of Tasmania; Malcolm Oxley; James Scott; The Petrie Museum; Noel L. Sweitzer; The University of Glasgow Library; Tricia Usick; Dr. Helen Whitehouse.

Finally, I should like to thank Renfrew District Council particularly the Department of Arts and Libraries under the guiding hand of Ann Saunders for supporting the publication, Bill Campbell and Mainstream Publishing and most importantly my wife, Jacqueline who has at times wondered if she was married to Arthur Mace.

Dr. Christopher C. Lee
Lochwinnoch
October 1992

# Contents

**Preface**
11

**Foreword**
by Marsha Hill,
Department of Egyptian Art,
Metropolitan Museum of Art, New York
13

Chapter One
**A Country Childhood**
15

Chapter Two
**With 'the great man'**
31

Chapter Three
**'The ideal excavator'**
57

Chapter Four
**'It takes one's breath away'**
81

Chapter Five
**'A beautiful wonderful party ...'**
113

Chapter Six
**After Tutankhamun**
137

References
151

Bibliography and Sources
157

Index
159

Mrs. W. M. MACE
Deceased.

# Preface

In the spring of 1989 the archives of Egyptologist Arthur C. Mace (1874–1928) came to light in the small Scottish village of Lochwinnoch about 11 miles south west of the town of Paisley. Almost forgotten since 1928 these papers told the story of an important, but neglected figure of twentieth-century archaeology.

Mace learnt his skills under the guidance of Flinders Petrie, became a valued member of the Hearst funded expedition for the University of California, and one of the founding members of the Department of Egyptian Art at New York's Metropolitan Museum. At the Metropolitan he was, especially in the beginning, the guiding hand behind the department's fieldwork. He discovered the tomb of Senebtisi with its beautiful Middle Kingdom jewellery and he skillfully reconstructed the jewel caskets of the Lahun princess. In 1922 he was seconded to work with Howard Carter on the tomb of Tutankhamun where he played a major role that has not been fully acknowledged. The preservation of many of the Tutankhamun objects in Cairo was due to the on-site restoration carried out by Mace.

The Mace papers came to light because of a request by school-children in the village of Lochwinnoch that their local museum should produce 'an exhibition about ancient Egyptians'. A subsequent remark to a local lady brought the response, 'Perhaps you might be interested in some things I have at home for your exhibition, you see my father was an Egyptologist, you won't know of him, Arthur Mace, he's long forgotten'. This was Mrs. Margaret Orr, an elegant and cultured lady, known for her love of music and country life. In an attic which might well have been a stage setting, among the old deck chairs, straw hats, train set and collection of shells was a black deed box with gold letters labelled 'Mrs. W. M. Mace Deceased'. In the box were letters, diaries and journals telling the story of a young man who first went to Egypt in 1897. There was also a handwritten manuscript of ten chapters by Arthur Mace for *The Tomb of Tutankhamun*, a book popularly ascribed to Howard Carter. There were many photographs giving a vivid social picture of life in Egypt during the early twentieth-century, one was particularly strange; it showed a group of Egyptians holding a large wooden box outside a mud house. 'What's this?' Mrs. Orr was asked; 'That's my mother's Bechstein grand piano you know ... it came by camel'.

*Margaret Orr's attic at Lochwinnoch. (From the collections of the Department of Arts & Libraries, Renfrew District Council. Photograph by Jim Hermit)*

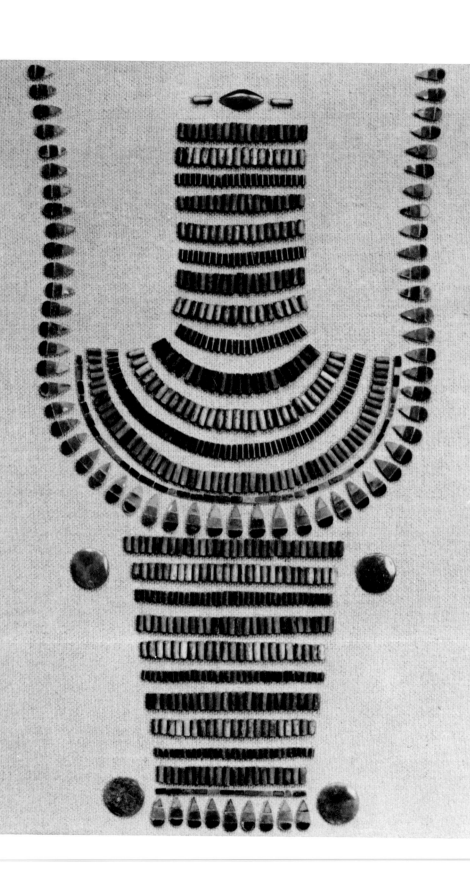

# Foreword

By Marsha Hill
Department of Egyptian Art, Metropolitan Museum of Art, New York

---

Arthur Mace was one of the generation of excavators who were trained by Petrie and then went on to help establish new outposts of scientific archaeology. Mace joined the Metropolitan Museum's new Egyptian Expedition and Egyptian Art Department.

In those busy and exciting early days, Mace helped to evolve comprehensive plans for the Expedition's excavations and to establish its procedures and recording systems. He himself excavated the major site of the North Pyramid and associated cemetery at Lisht, uncovering important information and multitudes of significant and often beautiful objects which are today in Cairo and New York. In the Museum, he worked on our first planned installation of Egyptian art, and with his own hands restored the cosmetic boxes of Princess Sithathoryunet from Lahun, one of the treasures of the Egyptian Art Department.

The imprint of Mace's meticulous, analytical, and artistic approach can be found throughout the collection. Outside those familiar with the history of that collection, however, his work is not so well-known. His two years of hard labour in the salvaging of Tutankhamun's treasures tend to be obscured in the glory of the find itself. And his own major excavations at Lisht North were not completed or published in final reports by the time of his death, partly because of Tutankhamun, partly because of his failing health, but also partly because the huge archaeological undertakings of the era were almost beyond the strength of a single individual to complete. Only today can we foresee that Mace's archaeological work will be completed - the Lisht North cemetery by Janine Bourriau, the pyramid itself by Dieter Arnold, and the village by Felix Arnold.

So it is gratifying that now with Christopher Lee's most attentive and detailed biography of Mace, following on an exhibition organized by Dr. Lee for Lochwinnoch and Paisley, Arthur Mace's extensive contributions are becoming more widely known. Even more compellingly, through Dr. Lee's thoughtful examination of the life of this early Egyptologist we begin to comprehend the goals, opportunities, costs, and rewards of those early days at the frontiers of a new endeavour.

*A bead panel from the inner coffin of Senebtisi. (Courtesy of the Metropolitan Museum of Art, New York, acc. no. 07.227.6-7, Rogers Fund 1907)*

*The Mace family c. 1890. The
Reverend John Mace and his
wife Mary Ellen (Minna) with
their children. Arthur Mace is
bearded and wearing a hat,
already he looked the budding
archaeologist. (From the
collection of Margaret Orr)*

CHAPTER ONE

# A
# Country Childhood
## 1874-1897

'...What gifts –
your fairy godmother bestowed'

*Arthur C. Mace, Tasmania, 1876. (From the collection of Margaret Orr)*

The early life of Arthur C. Mace whose death in 1928, at the age of fifty-four, was to be linked with the ever-popular curse of Tutankhamun, could not have been less dramatic. Indeed the world of the Mace family had more of the flavour of the novels of Anthony Trollope and E. M. Forster running through it. Mace's early years were inhabited by curates, wardens, rectors, rural deans and bishops. Family and friends had names which seem to come straight out of the *Barchester Chronicles* or *A Room With a View*, such as Dr. Pope, Alban, Bishop Abraham, Young Beeb, Jasper, Mrs. Dorking and Dr. Darling.(1)

In the complex class system of Victorian Britain, the Mace family were members of the English upper-middle classes. They were not wealthy, but as a clerical family had a degree of status and a certain entree into local landed society. They were genteel and kept servants. They were intelligent and informed and demonstrated in a patrician sort of way a grasp of social problems and a willingness to discuss social issues. An academic tradition in the family meant that great store was set by education. Arthur and his brothers and sisters were educated privately and the financing of this was often a considerable worry for his parents. In religious matters the Mace family was connected with the Oxford Movement. This was far from being a 'popular movement'; it tended to attract those of similar backgrounds in terms of class and education. They were High Church Anglicans and presumably, judging by the attitude of Arthur's

*The Reverend John Cruttenden Mace, Arthur's father. (From the collection of Margaret Orr)*

grandfather to the Liberals, Tories.(2)

Although he was largely brought up in Britain Arthur Mace was, in fact, Australian by birth. To be pedantic, he was a Tasmanian, born in Hobart on the morning of Friday, 17 July 1874. Tasmania was then independent from Australia. He was one of twelve children born to the Reverend John Cruttenden Mace and Mary Ellen (Minna) Bromby. Only six of the children survived into adulthood and in addition to Arthur there were Henry, Hilda, Christopher, Gertrude and Alban. The Reverend John Mace was the son of a Sydney Doctor, Henry Mace. He seems to have spent much of his time with his mother's (Caroline Cruttenden) family in Woodsden where they had a large sheep farm. According to a family story the farm buildings were constructed by convict labour. Originally both the Maces and the Cruttendens came from Tenterden in Kent.

An interesting account of life in Tasmania in the second-half of the nineteenth century is preserved in a journal from the Mace papers. The journal was written in November and December of 1864 probably by a visiting Mace relative and sent home to England. The journey from Hobart to Woodsden was clearly not an easy one:

> Reached Richmond, at one, partook of cakes and wine and started again in Mr. Cox's dog cart, he always drives tandem, it is really dangerous work along these rough roads. I had the back seat and was nearly jolted out of my life and was glad enough when half the twenty-five miles were past and Fred Mace appeared in the distance with a led horse for me. He said I looked like a ghost and I really did not feel as if I could have reached the end of my journey alive.

Fortunately, it would appear that the lady found Woodsden worth the journey, it was 'such a pretty place and altogether the nicest house to stay in the country in my opinion'. At times the journal took a condescending view of the lifestyle of the visitor's colonial cousins; for example her view of the local parson:

> Mr. Dobson, the Parson is a great trial to them, a clever man but utterly inert, spends a great deal of his time in working a sewing machine and making pastry. I do think he is the oddest specimen of the many odd Tasmanian clergy.

If the parson could be ridiculed, then relatives had to be humoured, at least while one was a guest:

> We get the Miss Cruttendens to give us such little jobs to do as all the country ladies here go in for shelling peas, making cakes, picking gooseberries etc. One day I made two glorious loaves of bread and felt two inches taller at once ... I spend a great deal of time wandering about the house in a delightfully vague manner ... had great fun hunting for eggs. Every day at five one of us went to skim all the milk. Altogether I went in for truly rural delights. Despise them not my friends - such occupations are worth all your fashions and balls ten times over.(3)

Arthur Mace's first eight years were to be strongly influenced by this Tasmanian rural background and when they returned to England it was the country that Arthur's parents made their base.

Arthur's mother Mary Ellen Bromby (known as Minna) was the daughter of Charles Henry Bromby DD (1814–1907), the Bishop of Tasmania, and of Mary Anne daughter of Dr. Bodley of Brighton. The Bishop had the distinction of being the last colonial prelate to be appointed by Queen Victoria. With a classics degree he had a reputation for the high standard of his pastoral and educational work. An obituary cited among his achievements, the foundation of 'one of the earliest and most successful working men's clubs', as well as 'the renowned Cheltenham Ladies College'.(4) In 1864 he left Cheltenham where he was vicar of St. Paul's and principal of Cheltenham training college, upon his appointment to succeed the first Bishop of Tasmania. This appointment was encouraged by Anthony Ashley Cooper, the seventh Earl of Shaftesbury, who was impressed by Bromby's Ministry among the poor. He was consecrated in Canterbury Cathedral by Dr Longley, the Archbishop. Life in Tasmania cannot always have been easy as much of the work was undertaken on horseback over rough bush roads. Among the problems he faced during his episcopate was the disestablishment of the Church on the island. His episcopacy was also noted for the completion of St David's Cathedral in 1874 which was designed by G. F. Bodley, his brother-in-law. A Hobart lady described a typical service:

> The Church is so packed that you have to sit sideways-on to sit at all and people often have to sit against the wall or at the end because of want of room. There are no aisles, just the broad nave filled with chairs, and men on one side and women on the other. Of course the service is very ritualistic with all the accessories and very devout.(5)

Bishop Bromby was a vigorous man who earned respect and admiration. He was a man of considerable intellect and yet extremely practical. He was also tolerent, broad-minded and had a sense of humour. These qualities were inherited by his grandson. He wrote a number of educational and religious works and yet was equally able to cope with the demands of a poor urban parish or a rural diocese in the colonies that was almost the size of Ireland. Bromby was on the right of the Church and yet he encouraged disestablishment of the Church in Tasmania. He saw his role not as a member of the Church of England in the colonies, but as a representative of the Holy Catholic Church. He lived until the age of ninety-three and was therefore a considerable influence on Arthur who demonstrated many of his characteristics.

A family story suggests that when the Bromby's daughter Mary Ellen was being courted by John Mace, the Bishop's main concern was that his prospective son-in-law should have a respectable career. John was therefore encouraged to enter the Church. The family at Woodsden were very religious and indeed were largely responsible for building the local church. Nevertheless it is difficult to know if John's commitment to his new career was wholehearted. They spent the first few years of their married life at Woodsden, but with a growing family and the need for John to complete his

*The Mace family home, in Herefordshire. (From the collection of the author)*

studies for the ministry they moved to Hobart. It was during this period that Arthur was born at the parsonage in Glenorchy, a northern suburb of the city. John was to be a curate in several parishes on the island before the whole family returned to England in 1882 with the Bishop's resignation and semi-retirement.(6)

On his return to England Bishop Bromby served as assistant Bishop successively in the dioceses of Lichfield, and Bath and Wells. The last few years of his life were spent at All Saints Vicarage, Clifton with Arthur's clerical uncle, Henry Bromby. Even at Clifton in his declining years, white-haired and bent, he continued to preach. One of his last sermons was in the workhouse chapel on the occasion of the death of Queen Victoria.(7) There is some difficulty in putting a chronological framework on the career of John Mace in England. His time seems to have been curiously divided between various parishes in Herefordshire and London. In Hereford he was curate at Eardisley and subsequently Rector of Putley.(8) In London he was Vicar of Christ Church, Hackney. These must have been very contrasting appointments. Herefordshire was rural and Hackney was an area which contained a great variety of social groups. The north of the borough in Stoke Newington and around Victoria Park was quite wealthy, but to the south the area known as Shoreditch was very poor.(9) It seems that John Mace's work was in the less salubrious part of the borough with its poverty, slums, and the problems of drink and unemployment.

The spells in the country were by all accounts for the benefit of Minna's health. It seems she was not a particularly strong woman and perhaps after a dozen or more pregnancies this was hardly surprising.

Historians often talk glibly of Victorian infant mortality statistics, but behind the figures there was of course all the emotional trauma of the death of a child and the experience of numerous debilitating miscarriages. In the Mace papers a number of letters provide the qualitative side to the cold statistics. Thus a letter of 1878 from Grandmother Bodley begins:

> Dear Minna
> My letter this month must be to you, so much you have been in my thoughts since the last mail brought us our letters from you. Although I have never known the sorrow your heart is feeling the love I have felt for my darling little ones has taught me how distressing it must be to part with them, but only for a season Dear Minna, for such are the Kingdom of Heaven.(10)

On another occasion young Arthur received a letter from his Aunt Gerty:

> Dear Arthur
> I am afraid you are feeling rather sad today so I write you a little note to cheer you up. I expect father may have left you which will make it worse for you. I am so sorry you have lost your new little baby brother it is sad for you all ...(11)

Minna's weak constitution was further illustrated by numerous references in her letters to colds and chest ailments, influenza, Russian epidemics and scarletina. These concerns were accompanied by that Victorian phenomenon a constant preoccupation with draughts and chills and the necessity of wrapping up against them. The following were typical of comments in Minna's letters:

> A shivery cold day and I got a sort of chill at early sunrise, so John would not hear of my going out again.

> I spent a solitary evening very close to the fire.

> I spent a quiet day mostly on the sofa.

> I went heavily covered in shawls

> I am condemned to cod liver oil and mustard plasters.(12)

As a result of Minna's delicacy young Arthur was largely in the care of his elder sister Hilda.

Worries about health notwithstanding, Minna managed to provide a loving family home, foster an interest among her children in literature, and develop in them an awareness of social problems. Minna seems to have had that interesting combination of characteristics that develop with a scholarly nature and yet at the same time she was highly sociable and hospitable. Like her granddaughter, Margaret, whom she would never know, Minna liked to surround herself with interesting young people with ideas, talents or just a gift for good conversation. These qualities must have produced the ideal clergyman's wife.

John must have lived and worked very much in the shadow of his eminent father-in-law the Bishop. He seems to have been a jolly man, sociable like his wife and loving nothing better than attending village dances or a tennis party at the Rectory. He served his Church well and spent a lot of time visiting the poor and sick and raising money for local causes. At heart, however, he was a countryman and his interests lay in country pursuits like pig keeping and breeding ornamental fowl. He even produced his own pork pies which were generously distributed around the village.

Bringing up six children on a curate's income could not have been easy, but John Mace had little regard for money and even less idea of its value. It was probably just as well that there was 'a little private money' from the Bromby side of the family.(13) In any case Minna appears to have been a good manager and a sensible and thrifty housewife. Like many Victorians she put her skills as a needlewoman to practical use. Thus on 1 October 1889, she wrote:

> I devoted myself to needlework, doing up winter things and making a set of nightshirts for Jack ... had an old woman in three days to help and she proved very skilful and turned a coat of Jack's into quite a respectable one for Chris ...

The household economy was assisted by the gifts of local farmers and landowners. This meant that the family diet was often quite richly embellished and menus included rabbit, venison, pheasant and partridge. When out visiting, Minna always seemed to return home with jars of jam, fruit or honeycombs. For Christmas 1889 there was the usual gift of a hamper from 'the Bousfield's' which 'has never failed us since we reached England and enables us to do better than we would otherwise manage to do'. Minna described the contents in detail:

> The hamper contained among other things, a large ham, tins of soup and potted meats, mincemeat, and a huge Christmas cake, shortbread, preserved pineapple beside dried fruits and sweetmeats in great abundance, crackers, chestnuts, chocolates etc. and the usual tins of superior tobacco for John and a book for baby, also in another package was a Punch and Judy Show.(14)

Arthur's home life was evidently far from extravagant but comfortable, simple and earnest. There were few opportunities to be idle and there were always bazaars and sales of work to organise and money to raise for cabmen's shelters or lunatic asylums to visit. There were garden parties at the Rectory and tableaux vivants to supervise for the organ fund. Arthur was much lauded by his mother for the organisation of one particular fund raising event:

> There was 'Caller Herrin', Darby and Joan, Where are you going to,
> Come lassies and lads (just like Caldicotts pictures), Auld Robin Grey

and Mikado, a very effective Japanese scene, crowded with figures and some action introduced, waving of fans etc. and illuminated with coloured lights, it was a gorgeous finale, quite a transformation scene.(15)

In the winter they planned summer activities. Life was clearly not dull, although there were many serious discussions about subjects such as Christian Socialism and lively family debates on topics like 'my views of the future state'.

Perhaps it was to ease the family's financial situation that Arthur was sent at thirteen to live with his uncle, Henry Bromby at St. John's Vicarage, Bethnal Green. Henry had been Chaplain to his father the Bishop, in Tasmania and was an uncompromising Anglo-Catholic. It may well have been Uncle Henry who helped in part to finance Arthur's boarding school education, for in 1889 at the age of sixteen Arthur was sent to join his elder brother Jack at St. Edward's School, Oxford.(16) St. Edward's, or 'Teddies' as it was affectionately known by its old boys, was a High Church public school, of which Uncle Henry would have thoroughly approved. Its creation reflected the Oxford Movement within the Church of England and it had a close association with Keble College. It was attended largely by the sons of clergymen who like the Maces, could not normally have afforded a public school education. The school was founded in 1863 in central Oxford and moved to its present site in North Oxford in 1873. It

*St. Edward's XI c. 1890. Arthur Mace is standing third from the left. The team are wearing the school blazer which because of its red stripes was known as a 'rhubarb'. (From the collection of St. Edward's School, Oxford)*

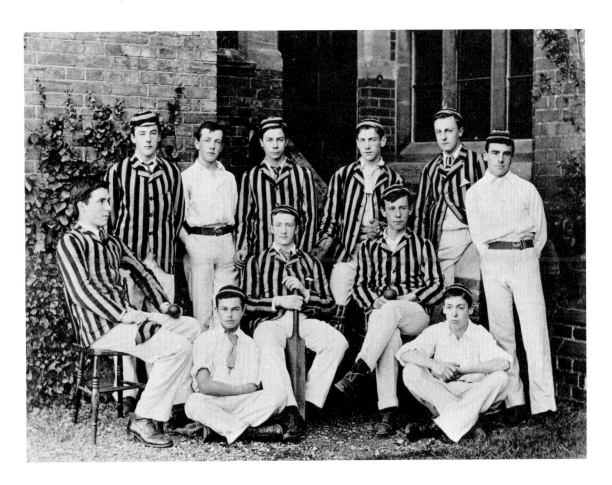

was financed largely by the private fortune of the Warden, the Reverend Algernon Barrington Simeon. An advertisement in the *Church Times* for 7 January 1865, read:

> St. Edward's School, Oxford - The object of this school is to combine careful religious teaching under a clergyman and graduate of the University, with a first class modern education. Day boys are not received. Terms including classics, mathematics, book-keeping, drawing, French, music and the elements of physical science, twenty-five guineas per annum: washing and the use of books two guineas extra. There is an excellent playground.(17)

The life of the school was surrounded by the services and rituals of the High Anglicans, with sung eucharists and an elaborately presented altar, processions with banners and the ornate vestments considered to have been ordered by the *Prayer Book*. As might be expected these developments did not appeal to everyone and the *Oxford Guardian* while commending the 'liberality and taste displayed in the design of the school' was clearly unhappy with practices which it considered 'simply plagiarised Rome'.(18) Even more worrying in their eyes was the appearance of the Bishop of Oxford at the laying of the foundation stone of the chapel which the *Oxford Guardian* regarded as 'a partisan function' appealing to 'dilettante ecclesiologists'.(19)

Real or imagined fears about the control of an Oxford School by the Vatican, notwithstanding, the school rules reveal a routine typical of public schools of the period. Life was spartan and strict. Thus when the school bell rang at 7 a.m. (6 a.m. in summer) a boy was turned out of his bed onto his knees by his neighbour to 'commend himself secretly to God ...'. Following milk (for those who had ordered it) there was preparation followed by chapel. Breakfast was of porridge, bread and butter and for those whose parents had paid an extra two guineas a term, there was meat, eggs, or fish. Boys could provide their own jam. School lessons began at 9 a.m. but even before this they were expected to have begun work on Greek translation. The day's lessons were broken up with sporting activities and meals. At dinner, joints of meat were carved by a butler and a cook and private bottles of sauces and pickles could be provided. Rather strangely perhaps, beer was allowed, one glass for each boy and two for seniors. Eggs could be bought and the owners name written on them. Full evensong was at 7 p.m. followed by two periods of preparation which was broken by a supper of bread and cheese. By 9.30 p.m. boys were in bed and candles were extinguished at 9.45 p.m., after which conversation was supposed to cease and 'no boy may get out of bed after that for unnecessary purposes'.(20)

At St. Edward's, life for Arthur was regimented and disciplined. Every hour of the day was taken up with lessons, sport or religious activity. Food by all accounts seems to have been plentiful, but monotonous and occasionally it required supplementation. In a letter written in January 1890, Arthur's mother writes of her childrens' return to school after the Christmas holidays:

> Arthur left on Wednesday 22nd, he took back jams etc., cocoa and condensed milk - these two items he bought with his own money to 'brew with', the boys two and two. They choose a partner for the term and make cocoa together, three times a week when leave is given and out come the spirit lamps and the

rest of the things and greatly do they enjoy it.(21)

This relatively spartan way of life and the need for self-reliance and various ingenious means of supplementing a tedious school menu must have provided excellent training for Arthur's later working life in the desert, particularly with that master of alfresco epicurean catering Flinders Petrie.

By all accounts Arthur enjoyed school and was a bright pupil. In a letter of December 1889 Minna writes with pride about her son's progress during his first term:

> In the printed list of St. Edward's School which comes out every year Arthur has more letters of credit after his name than any boy in the school, except the head boy - viz for Latin, and Greek Grammar, unseen translation and Latin prose ...(22)

Arthur also distinguished himself athletically; he was in the rugby first XV and the cricket first XI, a prefect and a member of the Field Club. Uncle Henry Bromby seems to have maintained an interest in his nephew and a letter written by him before Arthur's confirmation not only paints a vivid picture of a Victorian clergyman but also shows that much was expected of young Arthur:

> Only take care that your faith is real and that your repentance is deep and then you need never fear. Oh how much God wants you to be ready for the wonderful gift of the Holy Ghost. And he will help you lovingly to make your heart ready - Let me earnestly beseech you dear Arthur, not to come to God's altar with any wilful sin upon your conscience or with any wrong thing upon you that you are not determined to give up. I know well that school life is so full of terrible temptations - sins of swearing and lying and deceit do spoil the lives of so many school boys and lay up so sad a store of regrets in after-life. And then there is the sin of impurity which in so many causes does more harm than all the rest put together - Impure words and looks and reading and shameful habits alone or with other boys and an impure way of dressing. Alas! These things lay hold of so many and ruin them in soul and body.(23)

Uncle Henry's letter betrays many underlying Victorian middle-class concerns about aspects of morality, particularly those with sexual connotations. His well intended sermon must have conjured up a fearful view of adolescence for a sixteen-year-old boy.

Minna's concerns for her son were those of a boarding school mother rather than a vicar's worries about sin. In 1891 when Minna and John were living in Hackney, she wrote to Arthur:

> I often wished you lived at home, but perhaps school life is best, you have been a great comfort to us dear Arthur and a great joy and very little anxiety - I daresay you feel a little homesick at first, but plenty of work and play will cure that and please God we shall be able to enjoy our summer holiday together. Goodbye my dear boy.(24)

Further letters from Minna contain reminders to visit his brother at Keble, see

his sister Hilda, remember younger children's birthdays, help his father with a prospective choir outing to Oxford and so forth. Along with instructions and reminders were frequent admonitions to work hard. All this advice from home and the avuncular letters from Henry, combined with the rigours of life in an English public school, must have meant that life for this adolescent was at times far from carefree. If life was serious that is not to say it was dull or unhappy. In their succession of vicarages John and Minna provided a healthy environment for their children. They had contact with a wide spectrum of people from all social classes and lived comfortably. Throughout childhood a frequent visitor to the Mace household was his distant cousin and future wife Winifred and her mother Mrs. Blyth. In return the Maces paid visits to the Blyths at their home outside Walsall and the two families went on holiday together. Thus in January 1890 Minna noted 'Mrs. Blyth and Winifred came through to spend the day from Walsall, Gerty (Arthur's sister) and Winifred so happy together, over a dolls' feast and other delights'.(25)

The Maces and the Blyths were connected through the Newman family of which Cardinal Newman was the most prominent member. As a result of their church connections the Maces moved effortlessly in and out of landed circles, although their financial position was often precarious. The Blyths on the other hand, were a prosperous manufacturing family from the Midlands. Winifred's father, William E. Blyth, was the Managing Director of Windle and Blyth (Brace, Windle and Blyth in 1893) leather manufacturers specialising in saddlery and horse harness. They had large export markets in New Zealand, Australia and the West Indies. The firm probably originated in the early nineteenth-century; it was certainly the case that William inherited it from his father.(26) Mr. Blyth was a leading member of Walsall's business community, Chairman of the Philharmonic Union, President of the Chamber of Commerce, a Blue Coat School Trustee, Warden of St. Matthew's Church and a Justice of the Peace. He also sat for many years on the Committee of the Science and Art Institute.(27) Winifred's mother was a Newman from Cheltenham. A family story suggests that at the time of her marriage to William Blyth she was very unwilling to move from genteel Cheltenham to the grimy, industrialised black country, and was unhappy and homesick. Eventually when he became more prosperous, to please his artistic wife, William built a large mock-Tudor house in Highgate on the outskirts of Walsall. The design of the house was intended to create the illusion that it was much more in the country than it in fact was. It had large terraced grounds with a tennis court and a view over the hills. Although it was a large house it was not ostentatious by the standards of the time or the tastes of many late Victorian entrepreneurs. Indeed a description of it in *The Building News* suggests its interior was influenced by the Arts and Crafts movement:

*Mr. and Mrs. Blyth, Winifred's parents, in the drawing room at Crossways, c. 1900. (From the collection of Margaret Orr)*

The ingle has been contrived under the stairs, with open panelling and specially designed leaded lights. The hall will have a wax polished wood block floor ... the drawing room will have a floor of oak boards in narrow width ...(28)

Both Winifred and her mother were enthusiastic about art and artistic trends - they keenly supported Art Nouveau, William Morris and the Arts and Crafts

Movement. A photograph of Winifred as a young woman shows her wearing a dress made of Liberty fabric with a fashionable peacock design. Interior photographs of the Blyths' drawing room show the distinctive Art Nouveau fabric designs of Alexander Morton and Company of Darvel in Scotland, on an upholstered couch. The wallpaper in one of the photographs looks similar to one of the bold designs produced by Jeffrey and Company possibly from the Silver Studios.(29)

Mr. Blyth was a gregarious man interested in the arts. With his daughter he went to concerts and the first nights of George Bernard Shaw plays at Birmingham Repertory. As befitted a man in the leather business he was a keen horseman. William Blyth enjoyed travel and visited the West Indies, Egypt, Morocco, southern France and Italy. He was 'passionately interested in all things Scottish, particularly Mary Queen of Scots'.(30) William and his daughter toured Scotland visiting the sites associated with that ill-fated queen. Mrs. Blyth loved her home and disliked venturing too far from the confines of 'Crossways'. As she grew older the appeal of home and the lack of interest in the wider world developed into agoraphobia and her most ambitious perambulations were those from drawing room to conservatory. Photographs show Mrs. Blyth to have been an upright, well-corsetted, jet-beaded lady in the Victorian fashion. Despite her severe countenance her eyes betray a sense of mischief but the overall effect is rather stately and imperious. Her granddaughter has described her as 'a crashing bore' and perhaps when compared with the sociable Minna Mace, she was. However, Mrs. Blyth has an important role in the story of Arthur Mace, as it was to her that most of the surviving letters from Egypt were written by Arthur and Winifred. This was particularly so during the Tutankhamun excavation. It was also the case that Winifred was an important and influential motivating force behind the shy Arthur, who would have been a frequent visitor to the Blyth homes as a child and to 'Crossways' during his early visits home from Egypt. It can be presumed therefore that the influence of the artistic but forceful Mrs. Blyth and her educated, confident, no-nonsense daughter had an effect on Arthur from an early date.

Family holidays in which the Maces and the Blyths were often together were frequently at the seaside. A family magazine which Arthur edited evokes a charming picture of these holidays. Arthur wrote under the nom-de-plume of 'Acme' or 'Frog', his mother was known as 'The Duchess' and his father appropriately as 'His Reverence'. The magazine describes how the holidays revolved around picnics, croquet, 'scrumptious teas', rounders on the beach and 'paddling for shrimps'. On wet days they engaged in worthwhile activities such as compiling a geography book, reading French verbs and discussing the subject of old age pensions! Arthur and Hilda became so enthusiastic about their literary pretentions they resolved to become writers:

> Why shouldn't we publish our play ...? To which publisher shall we send it ...? I suppose it would be too great a risk to give up everything and take rooms in Paternoster Row and write?(31)

*The young Winifred wearing a dress made of Liberty fabric. (From the collection of Margaret Orr)*

In addition to writing short stories Arthur also provided the art work in the form of detailed pen and ink drawings. These were to prove useful hobbies. He was to find writing short stories a helpful diversion during his war-time service and was

*Winifred Mace (nee. Blyth) in the drawing room at Crossways, c.1907. (From the collection of Margaret Orr)*

to develop an interest in Egyptian literature. Drawing and painting skills were ideal for recreation but also were fine attributes for the field archaeologist in Egypt. As Minna wrote '... drawing and poetry what gifts your fairy godmother bestowed ...'(32)

It was probably in 1892/93 that Arthur followed his elder brother Jack to Keble College, Oxford to read modern history. Keble was the college with closest ties to St. Edward's and to the High Church movement. When he came down from Keble in 1895 Arthur was faced with the old family problem of money. The need to educate a younger brother may have persuaded Arthur to take up a teaching post at a school in Bath, particularly as 'reduced terms' for relatives were part of the terms of employment. Family correspondence indicates that Arthur was not particularly happy. On October 11 1895, Minna wrote to her son:

> Jack said you seemed rather oppressed. I hope it was only with a sense of responsibilities and not that you are not happy. I expect the work does seem hard at first and probably monotonous. You will soon fit into your groove I expect and after all Blessed be drudgery.(33)

As Minna tried to encourage him to stick at his new post she also put gentle pressure on him to consider ordination and a clerical career. Minna was a practical woman and realised despite her hopes that not everyone could have a successful clerical career like her father the Bishop. 'The clerical outlook' she wrote, 'is bad as far as livings go - men of thirty-five still as curates'.(34) Minna spoke from experience and life must have at times been frustrating for the daughter of a Bishop married to a man, who for all his good nature was largely unambitious and was more engrossed in his beloved pigs and hens than he was in climbing the ecclesiastical career structure.

The Church, however, was not to be Arthur's career nor was that of school-master. In 1897 at the age of twenty-three, Arthur left Bath for Egypt to work for his cousin the formidable Flinders Petrie, the archaeologist. Minna had some prophetic words for her son during his last rather dismal days in Bath; 'Never mind, providence has better things in store for you than anything you have yet experienced ...'(35)

*The family tree of Arthur Cruttenden Mace (1874–1928).*

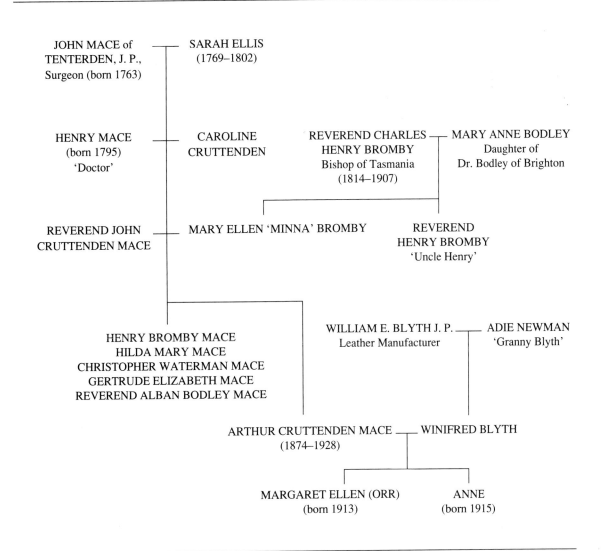

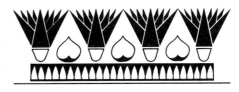

CHAPTER TWO

# With
# 'the great man'
## 1897-1906

Arthur joins
pioneer Egyptologist, Flinders Petrie

When Arthur Mace joined his cousin William Matthew Flinders Petrie, as
assistant, in the autumn of 1897, they had in all probability some limited
experience of working together. They were distant cousins, related through
Bishop Bromby. As there was an age difference of more than twenty years
between the two men it seems unlikely that they saw a great deal of one another,
although Mace's mother was good at keeping in touch with her extended family
in Britain and Australia.

Evidence of correspondence between Minna and Flinders occurs in a
letter of 20 November 1892, when she wrote to her son at Oxford:

> The other day Flinders Petrie wrote to ask if you were free and would like to
> help him pack and arrange his exhibits as he has been ill and must have some
> help. Fancy handling dear Kuanaten and the Princesses! It is a pity the offer
> did not come a few weeks later it would have been a nice occupation for the
> Christmas vacation and you would have payment. I wrote and told him you
> would be back for three weeks and that would of course be too late.(1)

*Flinders Petrie
(1853–1942), 'the great
man', from the portrait by
Philip De Laszlo R. A..
(Courtesy of Petrie
Museum, University
College, London)*

The letter indicates that the family already had some knowledge and enthusiasm
for Egyptology and were familiar with Petrie's work. Minna certainly seems to
have known something of his most recent work at Tell el Amarna as the

references to 'Kuanaten' (more commonly referred to as Akhenaten) and the Princesses demonstrated. It was here that the heretic Pharaoh Akhenaten and his Queen Nefertiti founded a new Egyptian capital about 1350 BC and established a centre for the worship of the sun-god Aten. After Akhenaten's death the site was abandoned and the centre moved back to Thebes. It was a vast and taxing site even for Petrie. Nevertheless he made a number of important finds including a painted pavement and a fragment of a wall painting. It was to the latter piece that Minna referred and it showed two daughters of the Amarna King, Neferneferuaten - Tasherit and Neferneferure. The painting had been part of a much larger composition which probably included the whole royal family.(2) Akhenaten's reign was particularly important for its artistic developments and studies of the female form are considered to be especially sensitive. The famous limestone bust of Nefertiti in Berlin is an obvious example, and Petrie's painting of the royal daughters another. It was in his own words:

> An exquisite group about six inches high painted so closely, like good Indian miniatures, that I was startled.(3)

In Margaret Drower's definitive study of Petrie she pointed out that the removal of this masterpiece on its plaster from a crumbling mud wall, challenged Petrie's ingenuity and patience. The painting was, however, successfully removed.(4)

The ultimate destination of the Princesses fresco was to be the Ashmolean Museum in Oxford but, first it was to be exhibited in Oxford Mansions.(5) With Arthur Mace nearing the end of term at Keble he would have provided a very convenient pair of hands for Petrie's exhibition. Certainly Petrie

*Princesses fresco, 1893 1-41 (267). (Courtesy of the Visitors of the Ashmolean Museum Oxford)*

needed all the help he could muster, as Minna had pointed out correctly he was in poor health. In fact he was suffering from exhaustion and stomach troubles. The digging season at Amarna had been strenuous and Petrie had also had a stressful period with the Egyptian Antiquities Service. There had also been bereavements with the loss of his mother and his friend Amelia Edwards.(6) Minna was keen that the relationship between her son and Petrie should be encouraged; she was clearly impressed by his latest achievements and went on to tell Arthur:

> I believe he has been made Professor of Egyptology in the British Museum, perhaps he will be able some day to get you an appointment. I do hope you'll not have to give up honour mods as that would give him a less favourable idea of your abilities.(7)

Minna was wrong about Petrie's appointment. In fact Petrie had just received the honorary degree of DCL from the University of Oxford but, more significantly he was, by the will of the late Amelia Edwards (1831–1892), appointed the first Edwards Professor of Egyptian Archaeology at University College, London. In the event it is not clear if Arthur did work on this particular exhibition but, it seems probable that other vacations were spent with Petrie. 'Young Mace' certainly attended the opening of the Edwards Library on 12 January 1893, and probably attended Petrie's inaugural lecture next day.

On 17 November 1897, no doubt well briefed by his cousin (Arthur had gone to stay with Petrie in the spring), he left England for his first trip to Egypt. He was to excavate for the Egypt Exploration Fund at Denderah, in upper Egypt, about forty-five miles north of Luxor. It is not clear from Mace's letters home, (which were frequently wrongly, if at all dated) whether he went by the quick route through the French Port of Marseilles or the more leisurely journey through Italy. In all probability he would have been anxious to be in Egypt well ahead of Petrie and would have been more likely to make his first trip by the fastest route.

A month later, Petrie, who was also travelling via Marseilles, was combining his journey to Egypt and his new concession at Denderah with his honeymoon. On 29 November, Petrie, now aged forty-three had married Hilda Urlin, a rather bluestocking barrister's daughter. They had met in the summer of 1896 when Hilda was working at University College making drawings of ancient costume for Henry Holiday the Pre-Raphaelite painter.(8) Mace was not only to be rather wary of Hilda, but also rather sceptical about her professed enthusiasm for Egypt and Egyptology. He would not have been amused to know that Holiday had painted her as Aspasia's handmaiden in the painting, Aspasia and the Pnyx.(9) Mace was interested in the artistic movements of his time and was also to become, like so many Englishmen, captivated by Renaissance Italy. He would have found it difficult to place Hilda Petrie in either context!

In typical Petrie fashion he and his Pre-Raphaelite bride arrived at Denderah by river on a small and rather dirty cargo boat. In fact as Drower relates they did not quite make it as far as Denderah and had to walk the last ten miles. On arrival at the camp they were met by Mace and Petrie's devoted Egyptian workman 'Ali es Suefi. Unfortunately, there do not appear to be any surviving letters or journals for Mace's first season. In any event he was clearly

*Hilda Petrie about to make a descent into a pit. (Courtesy of Petrie Museum, University College, London)*

the new boy. As Margaret Drower wrote:

> He had recently graduated at Oxford, and had no immediate prospects in mind but a hankering for Egypt; he proved a pleasant and helpful member of the team.(10)

In the publication of the work at Denderah, by W. M. Flinders Petrie, with chapters by F. Ll. Griffith, Dr. Gladstone and Oldfield Thomas, Mace was mentioned briefly in Petrie's introduction:

> Our party was happily composed. I had the advantage of the help of Mr. Arthur Mace, who was keenly interested in the work and most painstaking and thorough in all that he did.(11)

Another new member of the team who was to become a good friend of Arthur Mace and was also to work for the Metropolitan Museum of Art was Norman de Garis Davies (1865–1941). Davies, educated at Glasgow University, had long been interested in Egyptology but, had joined the ministry of the Unitarian Church and worked in Australia until 1897. In that year he left his charge specifically to join Petrie. Davies who was an excellent copyist was set to work on the wall paintings.(12) In the middle of February, the party was joined by David Randall-MacIver (1873–1945). Like Mace, MacIver was Oxford educated, he was 'good looking and well mannered', and his particular interest was anthropology.(13)

Arthur Mace and his new colleagues could not have secured a better apprenticeship. Petrie was already something of a character and is regarded as the creator of modern Egyptian archaeology and more generally as one of the fathers of modern archaeological methods. Petrie's concerns were not in the huge monuments or intrinsically valuable objects which had been the mark of early interest in ancient Egypt. He was, on the contrary, fascinated by the smaller everyday items depicting life in the early civilisations. As a result of his interest in pottery Petrie was often known as 'the father of pots'. This interest was to prove particularly important in terms of historical dating. The sound administration of a Petrie dig was also marked as a major improvement compared with his predecessors. Great attention was paid to record keeping, dating, cataloguing and methods of interpretation. As his biographer has emphasised, 'he established a system for tomb digging which was to set a standard for later archaeologists'.(14)

Petrie's high standards were adopted by his cousin who quickly grasped Petrie's methods of surveying sites and his developing ideas on the preservation of antiquities. Mace was also to become 'an excellent photographer'.(15) Life on a Petrie excavation was, however, no picnic and as another of his students T. E. Lawrence was later to write, 'a Petrie dig is a thing with a flavour of its own'.(16) He ran a strict and very spartan camp as the American Egyptologist Breasted illustrated:

> ... Petrie ... had a genial face, kindly eyes and the agility of a boy. His clothes confirmed a universal reputation for being not merely careless, but deliberately slovenly and dirty. He was thoroughly unkempt, clad in ragged, dirty shirt and trousers, worn out sandals and no socks. It was one of his numerous idiosyncrasies to prefer that his assistants should emulate his own carelessness and to pride himself on his own and his staff's spartan ability to 'rough it' in the field.(17)

Mace was most certainly not this extreme, indeed as a young man he was rather

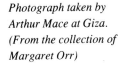

*Photograph taken by Arthur Mace at Giza. (From the collection of Margaret Orr)*

*Late nineteenth century tourists, assisted by local guides, climb the Great Pyramid. (From the collection of Margaret Orr)*

dapper in matters sartorial. However, his letters make it quite clear that he soon let his beard grow and that his hair became quite long. Later on he was to point out that in nearly every photograph taken of him he was pictured wearing the same comfortable Norfolk jacket.

Petrie's interest in his appearance was matched only by his interest in his stomach:

> He served a table so excruciatingly bad that only persons of iron constitution could survive it and even they had been known on occasion stealthily to leave his camp in order to assuage their hunger by sharing the comparatively luxurious beans and unleavened bread of the local fellahin ...(18)

Mace's daughter Margaret has said that he was often so hungry he had to smuggle food into the camp without Petrie knowing. Strangely perhaps, his letters and journals make only passing references to conditions. As his daughter points out, however, complaining would have earned him very little sympathy as he came from a family which disregarded such matters because they believed, 'one was expected to take without complaint what came one's way and make the best of a situation'.(19) During his second season with Petrie at Hu, Mace was moved to comment on a strange lunch of 'roast pigeon, tongue and apricot jam'. Petrie was said to be very fond of jam and his students would be expected to emulate his tastes.(20) In fairness it was not just Petrie's strange tastes and frugality which caused problems, but also the storage of food. For example at Abydos, Mace records having to hide turkeys on the roof of his living accommodation to 'keep them safe from the jackals'.(21) Despite the unglamorous lifestyle with 'the great man' as Mace called him, the fact remains that Petrie 'not only miraculously survived the consistent practice of what he preached, but with all his eccentricities ... established in the end a record of maximum results for minimum expenditure which is not likely to be surpassed'.(22)

Denderah on the east bank of the Nile was, as Petrie himself pointed out, known mainly as the centre of a temple and as the site of the cult worship of the goddess Hathor. The temple was 'one of the largest, best preserved and most popular examples of Egyptian architecture, visited and admired by every tourist, a stopping place for every steamer'.(23) More importantly from Petrie's point of view was that the view from the top of the temple indicated the existence of an ancient town, 'which is yet untouched except by native diggers'. It was also apparent that the inhabitants of the town 'were buried in a large cemetery behind the town which has never been touched by scientific work'. It was, Petrie believed, 'a most promising site for historical study'.(24) Above all, he hoped to find further evidence of the origins of the ancient Egyptians. They excavated in tunnels behind the dig houses and in the tomb pits of the cemetery. There were also some large mastabas (tombs of sloping sides and flat roof) of local rulers. Petrie also found the oldest known brick vaults. The finds were evidence 'that civil life and art continued in upper Egypt more or less unchanged from the Old Kingdom into the Middle Kingdom'.(25)

Arthur Mace's progress as an archaeologist must have been satisfactory. While the Petries went on a four day tenting trip Mace was left in charge and then during his last few weeks of the season Petrie 'left the direction of the excavations largely to Mace' while he spent his time recording his finds.(26) When the Petries made their way home, not this time by river, but on the new rail extension from Luxor to Cairo, Mace was left for a further month to pack

*Cairo in the late nineteenth century looking towards the pyramids. A familiar sight to Arthur and Winifred. (From the collection of Margaret Orr)*

*On the Nile, a sketch by Arthur Mace. (From the collection of Margaret Orr)*

objects. The packing cases arrived in London in the middle of June 1898 and Mace was there to unpack them. Many of the pieces not kept by the Egyptian authorities, were to find a permanent home in Oxford at the Ashmolean.(27)

While at Denderah Petrie had already decided that he would excavate at Hu during the 1898/99 season and hopefully he would be able to complete his dating system for prehistoric Egyptian pottery. Mace set out once more for Egypt, this time via Italy where he spent some time visiting Florence, Rome and Naples. In keeping with his family tradition, the journal was written as a round robin letter, which after circulating through friends and family in England returned to him as a permanent record for his archives. As the accounts were read by a number of people they were generally very circumspect.

Arthur Mace fell in love with Italy. In Florence, he spent five or six days visiting the sites and envied the students painting in the galleries. He saw Michaelangelo's statue of David, the Uffizi, the Church of Santa Croce and the Archaeological Museum. The atmosphere was heady and he wrote excitedly:

> This morning I found some glorious frescos of Andrea del Sarto's, in the portico of Santissima Annunciata. In the afternoon I went to the Pitti Gallery, the second of the large galleries of Florence. There they have some ten or fifteen Raphaels, several Andrea del Sartos and one or two beautiful Fra Bartolomeos. Also one beautiful Madonna of Murillo's. I have come to the conclusion that I like Andrea del Sarto better than anyone. His pictures are so restful and the colours so wonderfully harmonious.(28)

In Rome the Renaissance took second place to the ancient:

> Rome is different to Florence. The latter is a kind of Kaleidoscope of the Renaissance; everything one sees, every person one meets, remind one of it. One goes for a walk and here's a Madonna sitting on a doorstep the eyes unmistakably by Raphael. One turns a corner and runs up against St. Peter, a jolly looking old Priest, but what's he done with his keys? The very beggars at the Church door take their place at the side of the picture. Here the

atmosphere is absolutely different. It takes but a very small effort of imagination to fancy oneself in Ancient Rome. Fancy indeed I am in Ancient Rome. This very afternoon I attended an indignation meeting in the Forum moved by Cato Major, seconded by Cicero, that the custom of constructing medieval palaces from the remains of ancient temples was wicked and deserved the shortest censure ...(29)

In Naples, Mace spent so long at Pompeii that he became aware of the exasperation of his guide, but he was captivated by the place:

It is a wonderful place, everything is so complete, down to the ruts made in the road by the carriages. In the Museum are some of the bodies, all in the strained attitude in which they died; frightfully contorted some of them, with tightly clenched hands and grinding teeth.(30)

Arthur Mace never seemed to have enough time in Italy; he felt he was constantly rushing and always at the back of his mind, the thought that a boat was waiting in the docks to leave for Alexandria. During the First World War Mace was to spend more time in Italy and would come to know the spectacular Amalfi and Riviera coasts very well and during his long final illness, periods of convalescence were spent there. Italy appealed to the artist in Mace and his descriptions, with the grasp of detail, provide a clue to his relatively short but successful career as an Egyptologist. He was able to combine the benefits of an artistic eye and a feeling for colour and form with a practical common sense and a willingness to get to grips with the technical and scientific demands of his profession.

This ability to be adaptable to the demands of the work in hand will have suited Petrie literally down to the ground and for the second season of the apprenticeship Mace was given even greater scope and more responsibility. He was even acknowledged as a contributor to the publication:

In the preparation of this volume many hands have helped, Mr. Mace has written the account of the cemeteries which he worked ...(31)

The Hu site (also spelt Huw or Hiu), often known by its Greek name of Diospolis Parva, lay between Denderah of the previous year and Abydos of the following year. They worked first from Abadiyeh about twelve miles west of Denderah at the edge of the desert. They cleared the site for about three miles east and although the site had been plundered by dealers they found many hundreds of pots and stone vases. They then moved and explored the desert for two miles westwards. The party consisted of Petrie, Mace, MacIver, one of Petrie's students Miss Lawes, who drew the pottery, and Miss Beatrice Orme who with Hilda Petrie helped 'to draw the marks on the pottery and the slates and shared in the heavy work of numbering the skeletons and pottery and the general orderliness of the ever growing collections'.(32) The collection certainly was growing - by the time they moved to Hu from Abadiyeh they already had over a hundred cases of material.

Altogether they found a hundred and fifty new pre-dynastic pottery shapes to add to Petrie's original seven hundred and fifty. There was also some

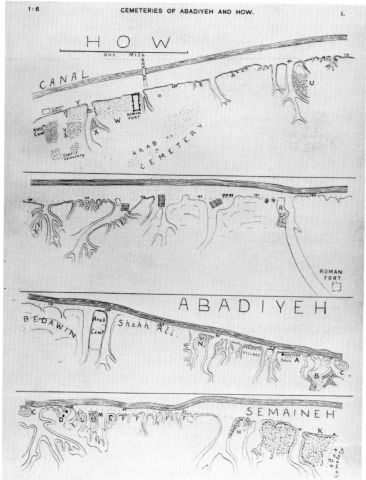

dynastic material. Mace spent a large amount of his time excavating the cemetery known as Y. He had to carefully avoid the nearby Coptic (early Christian sect) cemetery which was still in use. Mace managed to develop a good relationship with the Copts which pleased Petrie, and they let him work to the limits of their own cemetery. Mace began to worry that his relationship with the Copts was becoming too friendly as they became anxious to marry him believing he was 'quite old enough to have a wife'. Their well-intentioned matrimonial pressures were relaxed when Arthur told them that wives were expensive and he did not have enough money.(33)

Like all archaeological activity, Mace's work in the cemeteries at Hu was painstaking. He described to his mother how it took him four hours to clear a small, round, shallow grave about five feet in diameter. He had to work carefully because the grave was full of beads and rotten leather work.(34) There were disappointments: many of the graves had been plundered, and there were days when the seemingly helpful locals sent him on wild goose chases. On other days there was more success and greater progress, thus on 22 February he cleared, with the aid of fifty men, twenty nine skeletons from shallow graves and on 24 February he found a carnelian amulet with a gold Hathor head and

*Left: Sketch map of the site at Hu (Dispolis Parva) showing Mace's cemetery Y.*

*Right: Shabti (32717). Funerary statuette of glazed composition excavated by Arthur Mace, Hu 1898–99. (Courtesy of the Trustees of the British Museum)*

two scarabs. He also found an interesting burial:

> There was one burial in ordinary position, and below him were two more skeletons in a crouching position, the regular New Race style of burial. I think they must have been his servants or slaves buried with him to look after him in the next world; whether put to death for that purpose or not I don't know. It looks rather like it.(35)

There were some important finds including a dagger belonging to King Sewadjenra of the XIV Dynasty, which had an ivory crescent shaped handle and the nail holes on the shaft were covered with silver rosettes. Mace noted this find with great excitement and believed it to be 'the finest thing we have found this year'.(36) The dagger is now in Cairo Museum. In the excavation report Mace noted several significant graves including that of the servant of a Queen, Sit-hathor, which was eight feet deep, seven feet long and four feet wide and contained:

> The remains of a stuccoed wooden coffin, painted on the outside with

*Predynastic pot (30909). Decorated pottery vessel excavated by Arthur Mace, Hu 1898–99. (Courtesy of the Trustees of the British Museum)*

alternate vertical lines of white, blue and red; body straight out, turned over onto the chest, arms meeting together at the back; bones covered by a layer of painted stucco between two wrappings of cloth mask over face, covered with gold foil, hair in tiny plaits, one small glaze bead by the feet, another near the pelvis, by the left hand a twist of fibre, at the south east end a few gazelle bones; behind the head one of the ivory wands: the other ivory wand with a few of the ordinary pots, was found in the filling of the grave.(37)

*A watercolour of the huts at Hu by Flinders Petrie, 1898. (Courtesy of Mrs. M. S. Drower)*

For the most part the graves were of the very poorest people and contained little more than a pot or two and a few beads and amulets.

Petrie's team were well scattered. In the mornings MacIver went four miles in one direction and Mace four in the other. They took it in turn to take the horse. As Mace passed through the villages on his way to work the children yelled at him for 'backsheesh ya khawageh'(tip please sir); when they realised they were unsuccessful they had to change their call to 'ya khawageh bankrupt'(sir bankrupt). MacIver, it would appear was irritated by the children's calls for backsheesh and he took to chasing them, 'and when he catches them, which isn't very often, he whacks them'. The children got wise to this and led MacIver into a bog.(38) Work progressed well enough to let Petrie make several forays from the camp. There was a trip to Luxor and an exploring trip into the desert. Petrie felt happy leaving the work in the hands of his assistants and both Mace and MacIver were happy to see their boss take a few days holiday. This was particularly the case because they would be able to smoke in the dining room '... without bringing down on our devoted heads the vials of Mrs. Petrie's wrath ...'. Mace noted that the Petries' provisions included two camels, three donkeys and eight pots of jam for a six day trip. He was confident they would not starve.(39) Despite Hilda's involvement in her husband's work and her cheerful participation in his field trips with all the jam that this entailed, Mace was not convinced that Hilda was as enthusiastic as she liked people to believe:

> I wonder what sort of party we shall be next year. I don't think Miss Orme will come out again and I am quite certain Mrs. Petrie oughtn't to. She continually gets ill and has to stay in bed for a day. She doesn't like the mode of life I am sure, though she pretends she does.(40)

Although he felt sorry for Hilda he had to admit that they did not miss her very much while she was away. It also amused Mace that they always seemed to find the best pieces when the Petries were away.

By March 1899, the temperature was beginning to creep up. Work was increasing and Mace wrote home that he really did not have a moment to himself. There was a great deal of pottery which they tried to mark as it came in and there were as many as thirty skeletons a day to deal with. The pottery finds gave Petrie much food for thought about his theories concerning early Egyptian history. It was as Mace said a 'most curious cemetery in many ways' and he and MacIver indulged themselves 'in all sorts of speculations and theories concerning it'.(41) Theorising however had to take second place as they attempted to cope with the skeletons by putting them in each other's rooms. Mace was also given the task of taking down and preserving the plaster from one of the walls. The plaster which was covered with charcoal drawings 'falls to pieces as you look at it' and had to be removed piece by piece and put together on a sheet of glass with fresh plaster poured onto the back. Mace was not greatly impressed with his own work, but such delicate conservation work was very much his speciality.(42)

At the end of the month with the temperature in the 90s and a series of blinding sandstorms they began to pack for home. The dig houses were dismantled until only a room was left for sleeping in. Conditions worsened with the discovery of a hornets' nest and a plague of stinging ladybirds. While 'Ali packed the pottery, Mace saw to the more delicate things like a painted Roman plaster mask. This had to be wrapped in paper and cotton wool and then an old coat of Petrie's which, with the perennial problem of shortages of packing material, was the only thing available.(43) In terms of objects Mace did not feel it had been a particularly successful season. However, from the standpoint of historical re-assessment they had made good progress. Petrie was able to spend the summer on the chronological ordering of his pottery which he called sequence dating and which was to be one of his significant contributions to Egyptology.

Mace's last two seasons with Petrie were to be spent at Abydos with its vast and ancient cemetery area and its traditional association with the gods of the dead and in particular Osiris. As he wrote:

> ... a favourite place of burial from earliest times. Egyptians from other parts of the country, as well as the actual inhabitants of the place, had their tombs constructed there and naturally each tried to secure a place as near the Osiris enclosure as possible.(44)

Petrie had long wanted to work on this site which he believed (and was subsequently proved to be correct in his assumptions) had not only been ransacked by dealers, but badly excavated by Emile Amelineau (1850–1915). The concession was granted to Petrie by Gaston Maspero (1846–1916) who was just beginning his second period as the Director of the Egyptian Antiquities Service.

In November 1899, while Petrie was lecturing in Ireland, Mace set sail for the new concession and his last two seasons' work with 'the great man'. He began his journal on 1 November on board the *S.S. Congo* as the ship was passing the coast of Corsica. This time he was taking the quick route through Paris and Marseilles only stopping for a brief visit to the Louvre and to the theatre. The sea journey was quite rough and Mace was in a cramped four-berth cabin with '... one of the cut throatest looking villains I have ever seen'.(45) When he disembarked at Alexandria, there were a few hours to wait before the next Cairo train and he passed the time by shopping and purchasing a revolver. The question of security was important this time; the Abydos district was rather infamous as a place of violence where it was difficult to enforce the law. During the time that Mace was at Abydos an English resident and his wife were murdered and a pot-shot narrowly missed Hilda, so it was important to take precautions.(46) The ladies in the party were warned to take care and there was extra security for the dig house.

Before going to Abydos, Mace decided to make a diversion to Thebes which he had long wanted to visit. A delay in the train from Alexandria to Cairo meant that he missed the connection for Luxor, so he stayed the night in a hotel and dined with James Quibell (1867–1935) who had also worked with Petrie and was now an inspector with the Antiquities Service. The following day, Mace spent seventeen hours on the train to Luxor and on arrival at the station could not find '... a conveyance or a donkey, so I got a man to carry my goods round to the hotel', where he had to wake staff up. The inconvenience of the long train journey was forgotten next morning when he crossed the river. 'At last', he wrote, 'I have got to Thebes, and am happy'.(47) At Qurneh he visited Newberry, 'an awfully nice chap' and Spiegelberg 'great fun', who were working 'a magnificent site'. They asked him to stay a few days which pleased Mace greatly as 'Newberry knows more about Thebes than any Englishman alive'.(48) There was time to visit the great temple at Karnak and the obelisk of Hatshepsut. A visit was also made to Deir el Bahri where he saw Howard Carter at work copying the scenes and inscriptions of the temple. Mace makes no comment about Carter with whom he was to work so closely more than twenty years later, except to say that he thought Carter was doing '... a very good job'.(49) The two men must have got on reasonably well as they had tea together on two consecutive days. The little detour was completed by a visit to the tombs of the kings, '... which are quite as wonderful in their way as the pyramids. They are cut clean out of the face of solid rock, chamber after chamber, and run back, some of them to a distance of fifty yards'.(50) Little could he have imagined that one of these tombs would eventually be his laboratory where he would work with Carter on the tomb of Tutankhamun.

Mace intended to complete the remainder of the journey to Abydos by train. However, he was intercepted by 'Ali Suefi at a station half-way through the journey. 'Ali Suefi and some of the men had gone ahead by boat, and with little wind found their progress slow. They stopped to meet Mace who was delighted at their obvious thought for him and so he left the train and walked to the boat:

> The native boats somewhat resemble a Thames barge with a mast and huge sail. On the stern is a small raised deck, and on this they had prepared a kind of mattress, so I reclined in state while we drifted down the river, surrounded by 'Ali, my five Kuftis and two men and a boy who formed the crew.(51)

They made several stops as they drifted down river including one to buy one hundred and twenty planks of timber and 'five native bedsteads'. More stops were made for grass mats which would serve as doors, and sugar cane which 'we all chewed assiduously'. On arrival at their destination Mace found himself being entertained rather against his wishes by an enthusiastic local sheikh. Tired after the journey he was anxious to rest, but realised it would be unwise to refuse, especially when the sheikh offered to guard their stores overnight:

> We sat around a small table, and a tray was brought in containing a turkey, two basins of broth between five people, and a dish of a kind of stuff resembling - I really don't know what. Knives, forks and spoons of course we had none. When we wanted turkey we plunged our fingers into him and secured what we could.(52)

This experience was followed by an insistence that he stay the night and was even tucked into bed by his eager-to-please host. The following day work began in earnest. It took the best part of 17 November to get all the supplies and equipment to the site. Mace set up his tent and ordered ten thousand mud bricks for the construction of the camp. After sketching out the place of the houses on the desert, construction began, the walls being one brick thick. Mace began to have doubts about the strength of the building and was not at all helped by the criticisms of the locals. The bricks turned out to be so small that he had to purchase another four thousand and at one shilling and sixpence a thousand he considered he was being charged ruinous prices. Once the houses were roofed, the inside of the walls were plastered with mud. As the building proceeded he was able to look about the site a little and the comments made in his journal begin to show that perhaps Mace was feeling a certain frustration with Petrie:

> I have been investigating the ground a bit, whenever I dared to leave the men to build by themselves. All around the camp seems delightfully tomby, but I am afraid that is all Petrie's share. My part of the cemetery is some three or four miles off and I have not been able to get so far yet.(53)

By the end of the month everyone was anxious to begin digging, but Petrie failed to arrive and Mace became irritable, complaining he was getting fat with little exercise. A letter from Petrie indicated that the Abydos party would be quite large and would consist of themselves as well as Hilda, MacIver, a new assistant John Garstang, a maths graduate from Cambridge, and another Cambridge graduate, Anthony Wilkin. There would be a number of ladies including Miss Lawes, a friend of Hilda's who would assist with drawing,

Beatrice Orme and Miss Oldroyd. Petrie had been delayed by dreadful storms off Alexandria and meanwhile Mace was forbidden by the authorities to begin work without him. Eventually on 28 November, Petrie arrived with '... Mrs. in full desert war paint, Miss Orme and Miss Lawes; the two latter very short and in great contrast to Mrs. Petrie'.(54) By 30 November MacIver had arrived, they had reached water in the well and purchased food supplies. The serious work could begin.

As Mace predicted, Petrie worked the area immediately around the camp while MacIver was sent to excavate six miles south west of Abydos at El Amrah where he set up a smaller camp. Mace began work about a mile and a half away on a late cemetery. As they had all anticipated they saw plundering going on before their very eyes. At one cemetery Mace charged at a group of villagers digging merrily away with hoes. Most of them ran off, but Mace ended up fighting with one of the locals before he fled. If it was not the adults making life difficult, the children hung about hurling insults at him. This must have been rather menacing at times; it was certainly time consuming. In addition the outer limit of Mace's site was a four mile journey from camp on foot and then four miles home again at night. It was too far to return for lunch. His day could be quite lonely, although sometimes he had the company of Miss Lawes who drew the pots. Quite a lot of time was spent working 'new race' burials:

> These are very interesting to work. They are the people who used to cut up
> the dead before burying them, and apparently boil them, probably a remnant
> of cannibalism. They take a long time to clear and want careful notes.(55)

The work was painstaking and as always based on the principle of Professor Petrie's school that 'all results are untrustworthy or even useless which are not obtained by the personal observation of the excavator', or as Mace wrote in a less loyal and enthusiastic moment 'One day goes by very much like another'.(56) Evenings were spent marking bones although the programme was varied by moonlight walks over the desert which Mace made with Miss Oldroyd, whom he obviously liked. The admiration was returned:

> Miss Oldroyd took a lovely photograph this morning of two of my men
> sitting on top of a grave watching me clearing it out ... They are Sudan blacks,
> the most gloriously ugly old boys you ever saw, and made a lovely picture
> sitting there watching intently.(57)

The following day he quickly paid the workmen so that he would have the evening free for another walk. If romance was in the air there was little chance of a relationship developing as Miss Oldroyd left the camp on 3 February. Mace was up early to escort her to the steamer.

Arthur Mace's journals occasionally gave an insight into the relationship between the western archaeologists and their Arab hosts and workmen. As the comment on the Sudanese workmen above demonstrates, attitudes could be at once patronising but also affectionate. In later life, Mace was regarded as a westerner who had a keen understanding of the oriental mind. He certainly learnt to speak Arabic and seems to have inspired the affection of his workmen. When the Department of Egyptian Art at the Metropolitan Museum returned in

1985 to work at the Lisht site where Mace was to work from 1906 to 1922, they were surprised to learn that local people remembered their previous expedition, and even more surprised that 'the name they remembered was that of Mr. Mace'.(58) At times it was evident that the relationship between east and west was something of a game. If there was exploitation, both sides were capable of making the front running. Mace described how 'the natives' dealt with tourists:

> ... They have great ideas of looking interesting. One small boy I saw this morning had discarded all his clothes for the occasion and was going about in a grass girdle with a kind of green stuff around his head under the pleasing delusion that his appearance was calculated to wring backsheesh out of the stoniest hearted foreigner. (Howard) Carter, who is working for the fund at Deir el Bahri once saw a little girl plant herself down in the path by which the tourists were coming, deliberately arrange the pieces of a broken jug at her feet and begin to cry bitterly. Doubtless she kept the whole family by this contrivance.(59)

If the Arab villagers were capable of playing the system, they were also at times hard pressed to comprehend the activities of the archaeologists. By February of the first season at Abydos Mace had dealt with over a hundred and twenty skeletons:

> The Arabs have a very curious notion as to the reason why we take so many skeletons. They think that in England we are very short of men, and so being very great magicians we can take these bones and bring them to life again.(60)

In fact bringing the skeletons to life again was the least of their problems. They had first of all to be stored:

> We are so crowded out with skeletons now, that I have been compelled to give one important one a refuge under my bed. Now when I feel lonely, all I have to do is to look down and, the skull grins sociably at me through the bars of the wicker frame. Its quite company like.(61)

The season was producing a lot of material; Mace found 'a splendid bronze axe head', a 'nice bronze mirror' and 'a beautiful diorite shaped like a shell and cut very thin ... Mr. Petrie had never seen another like it'.(62) While Mace tried to cope with the finds, the Petries went off on their little trips. This was inconvenient in some ways as Mace also had to entertain any visitors who turned up, however, there were compensations; 'we smoke in the dining room and all sorts of wicked things like that'.(63) Davies and MacIver had become his friends. Davies he liked 'fairly' and MacIver he liked 'very much'. Mace was pleased to discover that MacIver was '... an old Radley boy' and that they had a mutual friend. The English public school system was useful - even in the desert it could cement friendships.

Friendships were also strengthened by breaks from the routine. There were Arab entertainments, games of hockey, visits to other sites and at the end of the first season at Abydos a trip to the Kharga oasis with Wilkin and Dr.

There we sat and waited for the
guard to find us, which he presently
did, very much out of breath, and having
evidently been looking all over the temple
for us. The crowd of beggars and people
who frequent the temple on tourist days
evidently know us now, for they content
themselves with saying 'good morning' and
make no attempt to get anything out of
us. This afternoon we went down for
our bathe in the Nile, where we were
again much plagued by the population.
We are so crowded out with skeletons
now, that I have been compelled to
give one important one a refuge under
my bed. Now when I feel lonely, all I
have to do is to look down, and the skull
grins sociably at me through the bars
of the wicker frame. Its quite company
like.

Feb 18th   Another nice false door turned

Myers. MacIver was called away to Port Said at the last minute and was therefore unable to go. They took with them a guide, two baggage camels, an escort of five camel men and Mace's own camel man Ahmed. As they set off Mace thought they made an imposing procession, '... first Wilkin hung around with knives and Mauser pistols, then Myers much behelmeted and bepuggareed; then myself'.(64) Travel by camel was a slow business and once or twice Mace was so drowsy in the heat he fell off. It took them about five days to reach Kharga and on the way there was plenty of interest to see, including a Roman fort, numerous Coptic remains, and by a spring of water, evidence of worked palaeolithic flints showing a halting place in constant use since prehistoric times. At the oasis they were met by the Omdah, who gave them tea. The three young archaeologists found him refreshing after the Nile people, '... cordial, unaffected and so far as we could see, not at all with the idea of getting anything out of us ...'(65) In fact the Omdah was so friendly they had difficulty in getting away without offending him.

The oasis was a fascinating place and it was probably on the basis of this visit and a subsequent report to the Department of Egyptian Art that the Metropolitan Museum later excavated there. They found a temple erected by Darius and added to by Nectanebo, the last Egyptian King. There was a large Coptic cemetery with Byzantine architecture. One tomb contained very early Christian wall paintings. These they photographed. They undertook some anthropological work, measuring villagers' heads, as well as more leisurely activities like picnicing. It was an exhausting few days, especially on the way home when there were a number of sandstorms. Despite this they enjoyed it, '... it's a grand life up there on the high desert and so wonderfully healthy'. It was the very stuff of *Boys' Own* comics.

The second season at Abydos and Mace's last with Petrie was also highly productive. MacIver and Wilkin were again at El Amrah and Mace continued to work on the dynastic tombs, mainly in cemetery D. He did not find a single intact burial. The wholesale plundering which had taken place had made it very difficult to decide to which tomb any object belonged. 'This was especially the case with the ushabtis which were scattered all over the chambers.'(66) In fact so many ushabtis (small statues buried with the dead for use in the afterlife) were found at Abydos that the Committee of the Egypt Exploration Fund decided to make a free distribution of them to members both in England and America.(67) The end of season exhibition was a great success and very full of objects. The excavation reports were published in a single volume by the Fund and co-authored by Mace and MacIver. It was Petrie's policy to give his helpers every credit for their work. In addition to the physical evidence provided by El Amrah and Abydos, the Egyptologists were able to draw conclusions about the origins and development of the ancient people of the Nile. As Mace wrote:

*An extract from Mace's journal, Abydos, 17 February, 1900. 'We are so crowded out with skeletons ...' (From the collection of Margaret Orr)*

The evidence gained from the evacuations of the last two or three years seems to point more and more to the conclusion that it was in the Nile valley itself that the rise and development of the prehistoric Egyptians took place.(68)

Arthur Mace's own development as an Egyptologist was to find new direction at the end of 1901. After four years with the Egypt Exploration Fund under Petrie's guidance Mace left to work with the American George Andrew

*G. A. Reisner, Director of the Hearst expedition to Egypt, for the University of California. (Courtesy of Phoebe A. Hearst Museum of Anthropology, University of California at Berkeley)*

Reisner who was about to begin work at Naga'ed Dêr on the opposite side of the Nile. Mace and Reisner had certainly already met. Mace's oasis journal records that on his way back to Abydos he called on the Reisner camp, stayed over night, and '... spent the day lazing and looking over Reisner's work which is most interesting ...'(69). Reisner (1867–1942), born in Indianapolis was educated at Harvard where he became Professor of Assyriology. He gave this up to take charge of the Hearst expedition to Egypt for the University of California.(70) Reisner and Petrie appear to have got on well in the early years. Reisner used some of Petrie's methods and even some of the workmen trained by him. In later years their relationship was often strained.

It is hard to assess Petrie's judgement of his young cousin's work: his own letters and journals do not seem to record any feelings about Mace. Where remarks have been found they are brief and related to work. Thus Petrie wrote: 'Mace and MacIver are both grinding hard at cemeteries one east the other west of my work' and 'Mace has nearly finished all of the ground east of this, finding prehistoric cemeteries'.(71) As neither men suffered fools gladly it must be assumed that the partnership worked well. Another indication that Petrie regarded Mace favourably was the fact that he was angry at Mace's decision to leave him for the Hearst excavation and he even tried to prejudice Reisner against him. Fortunately, Reisner was Petrie's match and not a man to be manipulated, he said, 'There's not a single man Petrie's had, who stuck him as long as Arthur did'.(72) Indeed Reisner was so impressed by Mace's work that on a return journey to the United States he took time to visit Arthur's parents. Minna Mace wrote a description of the visit of the Reisners: she was clearly very taken with them:

> Dr. Reisner is really charming, a very able man, quite unconventional with a plain rugged face, a square bulgy forehead, very bright dark eyes, an ugly, firm but very kind mouth and the heartiest laugh one could hear anywhere. Mrs. Reisner I imagine was a typical New England girl - now she is thirty four - (his age also) and a pleasant mixture of extreme simplicity, self possession and bright minded interest in affairs...(73)

By her own admission, however, what Minna liked best about Reisner was his opinion of Arthur:

> ... don't you be afraid about Arthur, he'll come out all right - I knew pretty well what he was before I asked him to join my camp - and he's done more than I expected. He's earned his money well and he gets more than I did at his age.(74)

Perhaps the Reisner camp held a financial attraction for Mace especially after four years of deprivation with Petrie. Minna was certainly impressed by the financial standing of the expedition's sponsor. Mrs. Phoebe Hearst was reputed to have been left twelve million pounds by her husband and was also backing expeditions in Greece and Latin America.

Reisner began work at Naga'ed Dêr opposite Girga in February 1901 following information from James Quibell the Inspector of Antiquities that the site was being plundered. The site 'consisted of a series of cemeteries from one community covering a long period of time'. It was systematically excavated between February 1901, and March 1903.(75) Mace joined the expedition in November 1901, and was given responsibility for cemetery 3500, while Reisner worked on cemetery 100, and A. M. Lythgoe worked on the pre-dynastic cemetery 7000. Albert Morton Lythgoe (1868-1934) was to become a significant figure in Mace's life and work; he had been a student of Reisner's at Harvard and had also studied in Germany. All three men seem to have quickly established a good relationship.

The extant journals for the years with Reisner are fewer, shorter and less descriptive than those with Petrie. Reisner had asked him not to talk about finds, so perhaps he was more cautious; perhaps also there was a sense in which everyday events in Egypt had become common place and seemed not worth reporting home. It seems, nevertheless, that he quickly settled down to life in an American camp and was soon able to celebrate 'a festival which I have never taken part in before, Thanksgiving Day'. He described to his family how Reisner '... ran up the stars and stripes with great ceremony and this evening we had a great dinner consisting of turkey and a wonderful pudding'.(76)

Petrie had always encouraged Mace in the use and practice of photography. Reisner, if anything was even more enthusiastic about its use as Minna Mace wrote:

2. ...is to have a bit of the site photo'ed before being touched, then again & again at successive stages of the excavation till the results are laid bare, but in the last photo. the contents of each grave are photo'ed before being disturbed — and so with the next piece. Nothing cld be more thorough. The photres. will be arranged in the University. also models of tombs. as well as all the finds not kept by the Ghizeh authorities. He is very annoyed with Petrie about a letter he wrote concerning Arthur, in wh he seemed to wish to prejudice Dr M. agst him — "I showed him plainly what I thought" — he said — "he didn't do himself any good by that move. There's not a single man Petrie's had who stuck to him as long as Arthur did." — I am afraid it is not a case of "See how these Egyptologists love one another".

*Minna Mace's letter
reporting a visit from Dr.
Reisner (undated) c. 1902.
(From the collection of
Margaret Orr)*

His system is to have a bit of the site photographed before being touched, then again and again at successive stages of the excavation, till the results are laid bare, but in the last photograph the contents of each grave are photographed before being disturbed ... nothing could be more thorough.(77)

Reisner supplied Mace with a 'twenty five pound camera ... and all the latest improvements'.(78) Field photography could be quite dangerous; Reisner nearly killed himself experimenting with '... a magnesium powder apparatus for taking pictures in dark tombs'. The whole thing blew up and metal from a stove flew past him and embedded itself in a table and in the ceiling. Luckily he escaped serious injury with only a singed head.(79) They were not discouraged and the following evening having taken photographs all day, Mace wrote:

> ... went down into a dark tomb and took a most elaborate flash light picture. What with getting the camera fixed up, and sending to the house for a candle to focus onto and preparing my burner and magnesium powder I should think I must have taken half an hour, and then the whole performance was over, and I was nearly blinded by the flash and suffocated by the smoke I discovered that I had forgotten to open the shutter. These are moments worth living for.(80)

Despite being upset by the loss of his apprentice, contact seems to have been kept up with Petrie, at least in the form of letters across the Nile. Petrie had clearly got used to Mace being on site before him and making all the arrangements for construction and the hire of the labour force. As Mace told his parents:

> I got a letter from Petrie this morning and from its tone I gather that he is not so comfortable as he might be building his house over there, and that it has had some effect on his temper.(81)

If Mace's journal was less full of detail than it had been in previous seasons it was certainly more confident in tone. Clearly the student had mastered his subject. By the spring of 1903 Reisner was sufficiently confident of Mace's work to send him with a gang of men to begin work at the Pyramids of Giza. He felt rather pleased to be able to tell his family that they should send their letters c/o Mena House, Pyramids, Cairo, although he qualified his rather grand instructions:

> It sounds a very extravagant sort of address, but it doesn't imply that I shall be living there, they have a kind of post office attached to the hotel.(82)

Actually Mace was camping just beyond the second pyramid. The site was as he said rather conspicuous and attracted tourists. One tourist who was staying at the Mena House Hotel at this time was William Blyth, his future father-in-law.

Reisner's excavation season seems to have been much longer than Petrie's and this of course meant working in high temperatures, well over 100°C in the shade on many days. As Arthur confessed they all became rather limp and washed out and it became an effort to cut each other's hair. This did not stop him from enjoying the work and even taking on hard physical tasks himself like levelling the ground '... it's fascinating work' he wrote home. There was less frenetic activity too with long periods spent tracing and copying inscriptions and of course there was photography. Mace believed they were 'reducing grave clearing for photography to a science.'(83)

The work at Naga'ed Dêr still had to be finished and so after preliminary work, Reisner took charge of the Giza work, while Lythgoe and Mace finished up the work of mapping, planning, photography etc. at Naga'ed Dêr. At Giza the excavations at the Pyramids led to the cleaning and identification of the royal cemeteries of Cheops, Chephren and Mykerinos. They also examined '... the later cemeteries of the priests of these kings, and they accumulated a mass of material on the development of the mastaba, the masonary, the art and the burial customs of the period'.(84) Reisner believed that this work, '... confirms and completes the materials at Naga'ed Dêr'. In his report to Mrs. Hearst for 1903–4 Reisner described the role of Mace and Lythgoe:

> ... it was necessary for Mr. Lythgoe and Mr. Mace to remain at Naga'ed Dêr in order to remove burials already exposed, to make maps of the cemeteries designated 7000, 3500 and 200, to unroll and photograph the Coptic mummies and to photograph a mass of pottery, beads, scarabs and other small stuff.(85)

In the course of the work on the Coptic mummies they uncovered a large number of fine coloured embroideries which had adorned the tunics and caps of the bodies. Assistance with the work on mummies was provided by Dr. G. Elliot Smith, Professor of Comparative Anatomy in the Khedival School of Medicine. Mace's energies became devoted to the Coptic material which was dated by means of coins to the period of the Emperor Justinian. The antiquities found with the burials consisted mostly of bead necklaces, earrings, pendants, finger rings, bracelets and crowns. They were made either of bronze or gilded bronze. One strange finding reported to Mrs. Hearst by Mace was:

> Curiously, a number of the old Egyptian amulets (sometimes genuinely antique) were found side by side with representations of the Christian ones.(86)

Of more significance, he felt, was the wrapping of the mummies. The bodies which were poorly preserved, were prepared with salt and during the unwrapping they found numerous well preserved fragments notable for their decoration:

> This ornamentation consisted of coloured embroideries representing rosettes, conventional flowers, geometric designs and figures of cupids, animals and men.(87)

If the years with Flinders Petrie had been Mace's apprenticeship then those with Reisner consolidated skills and provided experience with a whole range of ancient Egyptian history and archaeology. Mace was evidently happy working with the Americans and he formed a lasting friendship with Albert

Lythgoe. This relationship was important. In 1902, Lythgoe was appointed Curator of the Egyptian Department of the Boston Museum and in 1904, left Reisner to take up his duties there. In 1906, he was appointed by the Metropolitan Museum of Art in New York to establish and develop a department of Egyptian Art. Among those he selected to work with him was Arthur C. Mace.

*Egypt showing sites (underlined) where Arthur C. Mace excavated.*

CHAPTER THREE

# 'The
# ideal excavator'
## 1906-22

Metropolitan Museum of Art,
marriage and the War

On 15 October 1906, the Trustees of the Metropolitan Museum of Art voted to establish a department of Egyptian Art. This step which was taken 'after careful deliberation' confirmed 'that the Museum intended to make full recognition of Egypt as one of the great artistic countries of the past, and to devote a proportionate amount of space and funds to the purpose of enabling our public to understand and appreciate its art'.(1) As its Curator they appointed Albert Lythgoe who had recently left his position in the Boston Museum. Lythgoe was in the words of his student and successor Herbert Winlock, 'an extraordinary person' who in a few years built up 'an outstanding department'. He was first and foremost an organiser and his staff were selected with great care. Lythgoe was noted for his kindness and while far from dictatorial in his administration, 'anyone who was foolish enough to cross his path in matters of policy ... was not likely to do so twice.'(2)

Once secure in his own position at the Metropolitan, Lythgoe invited Arthur Mace and Herbert Winlock to join him on the staff. From then until his death in 1928 Mace's fortunes were 'intimately bound up with those of the Metropolitan Museum'.(3) Herbert Eustis Winlock (1884–1950) was the youngest of the three men. He was born in Washington and educated at Harvard where by his own admission his early student days had been somewhat wild. At one stage the Dean actually put him on probation. Despite this his academic

*Mace at work at Lisht.*
*(Courtesy of the Egyptian*
*Expedition Metropolitan*
*Museum of Art, New York)*

*The Metropolitan expedition houses at Lisht with Arthur's beloved pyramid in the background c.1907. (Courtesy of the Egyptian Expedition, Metropolitan Museum of Art, New York)*

record was impressive and he was to become a considerable Egyptologist and ultimately Director of the Metropolitan Museum of Art.

Mace and Winlock left at once for Egypt. Lythgoe had a number of matters to see to en route and so it was actually Mace who submitted the Museum's application for the excavation concession at their chosen site at Lisht.(4) Mace also hired the workmen and, as he had done so many times with Petrie, built the mud brick houses in which they were to live. The Petrie influence was still strong, as Winlock was later to report in an account of the expedition's early years:

> In 1906 Mace brought to the expedition a fellah of the village of Kuft in upper Egypt, who had been an assistant foreman on Petrie's work. At that time all archaeological expeditions drew their Arab workmen from Kuft ... thus when Mace brought Hamid Mohammed from Kuft it was natural that he should bring with him a nucleus of workmen who had had experience on different excavations and who were all personally known to both Mace and Lythgoe.(5)

Hamid and his gang of Kufti workmen stayed with the expedition for thirty years.

The barely recognisable pyramids of Lisht are situated about thirty-five miles south west of Cairo. Both north and south pyramids date from the period known as Middle Kingdom (from c.2134BC–c.1797BC). The north pyramid is the burial place of King Amenemhat I, of the XII Dynasty and the southern that of his son and successor Senwosret I. The site was as Lythgoe reported, standing upon rising desert hills, about one and a half miles apart and a few hundred yards from the cultivated land of the Nile valley. By this time the sites little resembled the dramatic pyramids they had once been, having collapsed and then been quarries. The site had been examined in 1882 by Gaston Maspero, Director of the Egyptian Organisation of Antiquities and in 1894–95 by the French Institute of Oriental Archaeology in Cairo. Maspero had encountered considerable problems with the high water table, and the French Institute had concentrated on the southern pyramid. Lythgoe decided that they would focus their efforts on the north pyramid of Amenemhat, with its surrounding cemetery of private tombs. They would also begin work on the eastern side of the pyramid nearest the river where the temple had been and where they expected to find on either side the tombs of important court officials.

Albert and Lucy Lythgoe arrived in Lisht in January 1907, and were delighted to find the site was ready for them to start and he was able to report to the Museum's Director:

> Mace is carrying everything along and is losing no time in getting things into full swing. He is most enthusiastic over our new expedition, and I consider him (as you know) invaluable to us in the work.(6)

Using an Arab workforce of one hundred and fifty they began to work by building a railway from the pyramid to the top of a hill so that debris could be dumped onto a previously inspected valley below. Clearing the lower slope of the eastern side of the pyramid they soon found material from the Roman period. By early March Lythgoe was able to report back to New York that they were finding XII Dynasty material including a scarab inscribed with the name of Amenemhat I.(7) During the first season a major part of the mortuary temple was cleared and about a hundred XII Dynasty tombs investigated. Most significant was the discovery of shaft tomb 763, the burial place of a wealthy lady of rank called Senebtisi. As with nearly all the tombs it had been disturbed, but only slightly and it was to 'yield some of the most important results of the year's work'.(8) Mace and Winlock spent two months clearing the tomb, and a considerable amount of time conserving and restoring the jewellery and other objects.

Senebtisi's tomb consisted of a vertical shaft twenty-two-and-a-half feet deep leading into a large offering chamber with a small burial chamber beyond. The outer chamber contained pottery, mostly tiny model vases and saucers.

*A relief block from Lisht, depicting King Amenemhat I, flanked by Gods. (Courtesy of the Metropolitan Museum of Art, New York, acc. no. 08. 200. 5, ca. 1991–1962BC)*

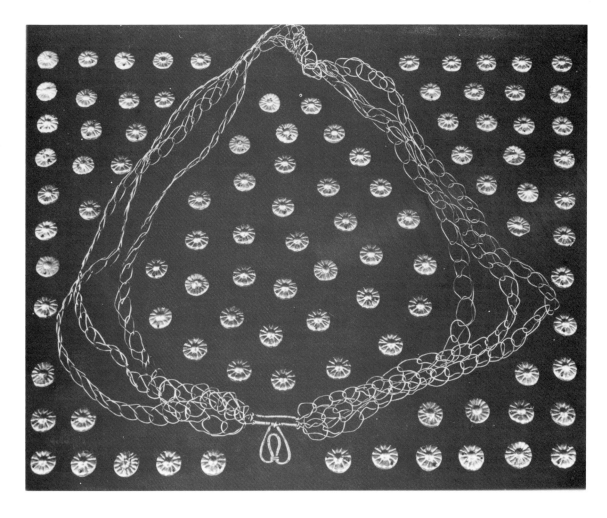

There were also several large dishes containing food offerings such as ducks and joints of beef. The body was contained within three coffins. The outer one was in poor condition and crumbled on touch. The second, of imported cedar wood, was in almost perfect condition. When the lid of the second coffin was removed Mace and Winlock found ten or twelve fringed shawls, each folded double and laid over the crumbling innermost coffin. The third coffin, in human form, had been covered in plaster and gold leaf. The body itself had been covered in pitch and within this pitch layer were found the most valuable of Senebtisi's ornaments: her jewellery. Some had been worn and some were constructed for funerary use. Among the most beautiful were those Senebtisi had worn during her lifetime, such as her wig ornaments consisting of 'a unique circlet of looped gold wire', decorated with ninety-eight gold rosettes. There were also two elaborate bead girdles one consisting of more than ten thousand beads and two broad collars of carnelian, glazed pottery and gilt plaster. The collars were not fashionable during the XII Dynasty, but 'the conservative, tradition-loving Egyptians ... provided funerary imitations of the traditional jewellery made of inexpensive materials such as plaster covered with gold leaf and faience'.(9) In addition there were necklaces and amulets as well as a small dagger decorated

*Senebtisi wig ornaments from Lisht, 1907. (Courtesy of the Metropolitan Museum of Art, New York, acc. no. 07. 227. 6–7, ca. 1850BC)*

with gold. As well as important artistic finds the tomb of Senebtisi produced useful historical evidence on the question of mummification. A long and expensive process had been used to preserve the body, hopefully for all time. Organs had been removed from the body and preserved separately in canopic jars. The body had then been packed with natron, a salt from Wadi Natrun west of Cairo. Once the body had been dried out with salt it was washed, cleaned with ointments, perfumed and wrapped in bandages of linen. The Senebtisi burial was important because it was one of the first recorded cases of definitely pre-XVII Dynasty mummification.(10) The body itself was examined by Dr. Elliot Smith who noted that Senebtisi had been a small and slender woman (about four-and-a-half feet tall) of around fifty years of age at her death. Senebtisi had a small face with regular teeth that had been kept remarkably well. Her eyes were large and her nose well proportioned.(11)

Mace's first season with the Metropolitan had been highly successful. Perhaps a renewed sense of purpose and a feeling of security lead him to propose marriage to his childhood friend and cousin Winifred Blyth. They were married in November 1907, in St. Matthew's Church, Walsall. One can only speculate about the feelings of Winifred's parents. They knew Arthur well, but they had both become very reliant on their only daughter's company; Mrs. Blyth because her agoraphobia meant she rarely left the confines of the house and Mr. Blyth because he liked his daughter's company on holidays and for visits to the theatre and concerts. Arthur was now making a name for himself in the archaeological world, but his lack of money must have concerned Mr. Blyth as a practical Victorian businessman. If marriage to an impecunious Egyptologist worried the Blyths then it clearly did not concern Winifred who was to take to her husband's profession and adopted country with vigour and enthusiasm. Winifred fell in love with Egypt; she appreciated the country as well as its

*A formal portrait of Arthur, probably an engagement photograph, c.1907.*

*Winifred Mace in her wedding dress, 1907.*

*(Both from the collection of Margaret Orr)*

history and customs, and delighted in helping Arthur with his jewellery conservation. A husband working for the Metropolitan, had its compensations. There were trips to New York, where she had singing lessons and spent her leisure time reading, painting, and feeding the squirrels in Central Park. Winifred's acceptance of life in Egypt did not mean she was immune from the difficulties that could face Europeans. For example soon after her arrival in Egypt in the autumn of 1907 she was ill; as Arthur wrote to Lythgoe: 'My wife got an attack of fever in Cairo three weeks ago and was in bed for a week, but has picked up again now.'(12) It was not, however, only illness that worried Winifred's parents, it was the lack of creature comforts and the embellishments that went to make up a good, solid, respectable, middle-class domestic environment. To ameliorate Winifred's perceived deprivation they shipped out a Bechstein grand piano which arrived at Lisht on the backs of baggage camels and was unloaded into the little mud houses where Arthur and Winifred lived. The Arabs must have found this very strange, but the episode indicates that even when living abroad, under difficult circumstances the British were able to keep up standards and indeed a degree of style.(13)

Following Lythgoe's plan of geographical and chronological excavation, 1907 saw the acquisition of a second Egyptian concession, that of the Kharga Oasis which eventually yielded late Dynastic to Coptic remains. This was the

*Having travelled by baggage camel the grand piano arrives at Lisht, c.1907. (From the collection of Margaret Orr)*

*Winifred and Arthur Mace at Lisht, c.1907. (From the collection of Margaret Orr)*

oasis Mace had explored a few years earlier and 'it is likely his first-hand assessment influenced the choice of site'.(14) For Mace the second season was to be spent excavating the northern side of the pyramid of Amenemhat I including the entrance. Meanwhile Winlock was to continue to excavate the cemetery of private tombs. Winlock had preceded Mace, no doubt delayed because of his marriage, and had undertaken some further camp building and had in Mace's words 'made a fine job of it'.(15) That year they employed three hundred men at the start of excavations before reducing numbers to a hundred. The large workforce quickly cleared the entrance to the tomb of the King and found a large red granite stela (upright inscribed monument).(16) Finding a way into the tomb proved more problematic than anticipated with the discovery that the shaft leading from the upper chamber in the pyramid to Amenemhat's burial chamber was full of water. The reason for this was that the level of the Nile was higher than in ancient times, and the depth of the shaft such that hand pumping was out of the question. The work would have to be postponed until the following season when more sophisticated pumping equipment could be employed.(17) In fact the problem with flooding was such that it has never been possible to investigate the burial chamber As Mace was to report in October 1908 the work on the pyramid graphically showed the amount of damage Egyptian monuments suffered in ancient times. Amenemhat's pyramid had become a ruin a thousand years after his death. Equally, just as the pyramid was used as a quarry by local inhabitants, it was itself constructed by stone plundered from elsewhere. The King evidently used material from the Old Kingdom probably in Medum or Dahshur. While Mace worked on the north pyramid during 1907-8 Lythgoe began to investigate the southern of Lisht's two pyramids.

By the third season the workload at Lisht and Kharga was such that the Museum increased the expedition staff to a total of six members, including W. J. Jones to record architectural material and F. L. Unwin to assist Norman de Garis Davies with the copying of Theban Tombs. The Museum President J. Pierpont Morgan visited both Kharga and Lisht. Mace worked to the west of the pyramid, cleaning XII Dynasty tombs and there was preliminary work on the temple and causeway of Lythgoe's pyramid.(18)

While members of the Metropolitan team had clearly defined areas of responsibility in terms of excavation, in these early days of the department the organisation of the work was largely informal. Lythgoe tended to take charge of financial and administrative affairs and Mace, with his experience of surveying and knowledge of conservation techniques, was left to organise the field work. After his death Winlock was to appraise the importance of Mace's role in these early years: 'to him more than anyone else is due the field organisation of the Metropolitan Museum of Art Expedition'. Mace hired and trained the Arab workmen, began record keeping and 'set a standard which his successors can do no more than imitate'.(19) In addition he was, according to Winlock:

> ... conscientious and painstaking in his scientific work far beyond the average, energetic and tireless in his attention to the detail of running a job and possessing the unlimited confidence of his workmen, he made the ideal excavator.(20)

The organisation of the Arab workforce was vital to the success of the expedition. As it has already been noted Mace encouraged the use of workmen from the village of Kuft. These men were divided into companies, each with a head man. At each of the sites locals were also employed to dig, push the cars along the railway and there were boys to carry baskets. Each company of men was paid a bonus for objects found and this was divided among them. Each of the archaeologists was assigned two or three boys to carry cameras and to help with the surveying and photography. Both Mace and Lythgoe were expert photographers and under their guidance some of the boys became very skillful. One of Mace's boys became an assistant foreman.(21)

In the spring of 1909 Arthur Mace was promoted to Assistant Curator of Egyptian Art. This new appointment meant he had to play a large part in the curatorial and administrative running of the department and so the next years were spent in New York at the Metropolitan on Fifth Avenue. Winifred went with him and they made their temporary home in Manhattan. Lythgoe was preparing the new Egyptian wing in the Museum and Mace's artistic eye was to be very useful. As Winlock wrote:

> Moreover to his fertile ingenuity were due many of the methods adopted in the Museum in New York for the exhibition of the Egyptian Collection.(22)

It would certainly seem that his ideas about display and interpretation were advanced for the time. As he wrote to Winlock in March 1910 from New York:

> We have a new scheme of arrangement here, and that is to expel the recent accessions from our wing and use the room for a slide show, outside the general chronological arrangement, illustrating the everyday life of Egyptian agriculture, manufacture, hunting, etc. We think it would make a thundering interesting room in itself, and it would also relieve our collection of various oddments that would otherwise have to be shown in kind of hotch potch cases. The things shown could be grouped under headings such as agriculture, building, war and hunting, industrial arts, household and personal, games and toys and so on. The walls can have large size drawings from the tombs illustrating the material and in the windows we might have positives showing similar scenes in the life of the modern Egyptians. It would also be nice in the cases where the modern implements resemble the old ones to show them alongside. Don't you think such a room could be made very attractive?(23)

The influence of Petrie in everyday objects had clearly been important. The interest in visual aids and the understanding that objects need to be made relevant to the general public is quite remarkable for 1910. Indeed, eighty years on many museums have failed to achieve this.

In New York Arthur Mace was also given the responsibility for the classification and cataloguing of the Murch Collection, the major part of which was presented to the Museum in 1910 by Miss Helen Miller Gould. As Mace told Winlock:

> I suppose Lythgoe told you about Miss Gould giving us the Murch collection; which commits of between two and three thousand objects. It is fine to have it, but, it will add to the length of time of course that this business takes.(24)

This important collection had been formed by Dr Chauncey Murch (1856–

*The Metropolitan Museum of Art, for whom Mace worked from 1906–1928. (Courtesy of the Metropolitan Museum of Art, New York)*

1907), who had been responsible for twenty years for the American Presbyterian Mission at Luxor. As Mace commented:

> Having a considerable knowledge of Egyptian Antiquities and a keen discrimination, particularly for dated pieces, he was able to make full use of this opportunity and in the course of time accumulated a most valuable collection of the smaller classes of material.(25)

Of most significance historically were the Murch seals and scarabs. As Mace wrote:

> In the daily life of the Egyptian the seal played an important part, and was used for a variety of objects. It was carried about on the person doubtless as it is today, as a means of identification and to be affixed to documents ... but in addition ... at a time when locks and keys were non-existent, it provided the Egyptian with a means of safeguarding his property, and we find that wine jars and other vessels, bags and boxes, entrances to tombs and even the door of storerooms and houses were all secured from theft or disturbance by means of the seal.(26)

Being at the Metropolitan gave Arthur Mace the time and opportunity to begin work on the publication of the Senebtisi findings and also to prepare the Middle Kingdom section of the department's handbook which would accompany the opening of the new Department of Egyptian Art. This took place on Monday, 6 November 1911. The new wing was opened with a private view for members of the Museum who were welcomed by the President J. P. Morgan. The Bulletin of the Metropolitan was able to report that the department's collection had grown to such an extent in five years that whereas it could formerly be accommodated in a single corridor it now required ten galleries.(27) The work on the Senebtisi publication took place more slowly; not only had there been all the work for the new galleries and the Murch collection, but from 1911 to 1912 Mace was in charge of the department while Lythgoe was in Egypt. It was also the case that Mace did not believe in the hurried publication of findings. It became one of Mace's ground rules for excavations shared at the time by the Metropolitan, that the publication of findings was left until the complete excavation of a site or part of a site had taken place. In this he was probably influenced by Reisner, for certainly this was in complete contrast with Petrie who believed in quick and cheap publications. For this reason when Mace died he had not completed any of the larger publications on which he was engaged, except for Senebtisi. In his aim for quality and perfection Mace ensured that outside his own department, he was, in terms of Egyptology, a forgotten man. It is a fact, as a prominent Egyptologist has said that, 'you are known in Egyptology not by what you do, but by what you publish'.(28)

After three years in the United States it was back to fieldwork and to Lisht in 1912. That year also saw the first mention of Mace's health when he wrote of bronchitis in a letter to the Metropolitan. The season was spent mainly on plans and notes for the pyramid cemetery of Amenemhat and on the Senebtisi publication. He and Lythgoe were joined in that year by Ambrose Lansing, a young graduate from an American college with no digging

*Arthur Mace with his elder daughter Margaret, c.1913. (From the collection of Margaret Orr)*

experience, but a knowledge of Arabic and a childhood spent in Egypt. Since 1910 Winlock had been in Luxor.

On the domestic front there was rejoicing, as on 22 February 1913, Winifred gave birth to their first daughter. Arthur Mace wrote to Miss Caroline Ransom, a colleague in New York:

> I know both you and Mrs. Ransom will be interested to hear that our little daughter arrived Saturday, such a fine strong girl, she and Winifred are both going on splendidly.(29)

The little girl, a strong determined child, adored by her parents, was christened Margaret Ellen.

As the political situation in Europe began to move inexorably towards catastrophe throughout 1913 and 1914, Mace returned once more to Lisht. This last pre-war expedition was a large scale excavation in which he began work on the south east corner of the pyramid in the hope of finding the tombs of important officials.(30) Again railway lines were used to dispose of large amounts of debris. As in the past there were problems with water. Fortunately they had an eight horsepower boiler and a two-inch pulsometer which with the aid of a Greek mechanic from Cairo, Mace believed would take care of any water that might be encountered. In fact the inflow of water in the chambers was so great that the pump was not enough and a second had to be borrowed from the Egyptian Public Works Department. A frustrated Mace wrote that on excavations, life was finely balanced between a state of 'hope and disappointment'. It could also at times be very dangerous and Mace risked his life investigating waterlogged tombs:

> Later when the passage was clear of water I had occasion for measuring
> purposes to crawl down myself, and found it no easy matter. I preferred not
> to think what it must have felt like under water, with the possibility of being
> brought up short at any moment, by something which blocked the passage,
> and prevented any movement either way.(31)

Arthur Mace's excavations at Lisht were to be hampered by more than water over the next few years as first of all Europe and then America became embroiled in the throes of the First World War. At the outbreak of war in August 1914, Mace was in London. He and Winifred with their young daughter had made their home at 14 Hill Street in St. John's Wood. Like everyone else Mace shared the belief that the war would be over by Christmas, as he wrote to Lythgoe:

> I don't believe this thing will last very long - all Europe will starve if it does,
> but it may go on into the winter.(32)

Lythgoe's reply expresses his concern for the prospects of the excavation as a long term war would make it almost impossible to send men and their wives to Egypt. Lythgoe hoped that the situation would not get any worse and that if Turkey stayed out he might be able to send out one or two of the younger men, if only to retrieve their plans and records.(33) As their correspondence at the time showed, Lythgoe was something of a worrier, not for himself personally, but rather for the common good of the expedition. Also, a man with worries was Lindsley Hall the expedition's draughtsman, who was also in London at the outbreak of the war. Hall was evidently rather timid and never completely comfortable in Egypt. Mace, in the spirit of his class and background, at once became a special constable and hoped to enlist; he was somewhat scathing about poor Lindsley's discomfort at being so close to the hostilities:

> The gentle Lindsley is in London. He underwent incredible dangers and
> hardships on the way from Paris to London. He now telephones me at
> intervals for advice.(34)

and on 3 September 1914:

> Hall is in Carlisle as far from the fighting as possible.(35)

Perhaps it was the tensions and uncertainty of war-time but if Mace could be irritated by Lindsley Hall then he could, as his correspondence to Lythgoe at this time shows, be quite exasperated by others, especially Winlock. The relationship with Winlock seems at times to be strangely inconsistent.

Winlock was ten years younger than Mace and ten years less experienced and yet he had been appointed Assistant Curator at the same time as Mace, and from 1910 was in charge of the Museum's work in Luxor. Possibly Mace's exasperation was that of the more experienced and older man. Perhaps it was a touch of jealousy in the face of Winlock's rapid progress. Arthur's tone could be quite churlish towards Herbert, thus in a letter of 19 January he corrected Winlock's description of the embalming process and then expressed his dislike of a particular chapter, 'so horribly reminiscent of Petrie'. On 2 December 1914, Mace wrote to Lythgoe about Winlock's chapter in *The Tomb of Senebtisi at Lisht* :

> I have made a few tentative corrections in Winlock's chapter. He has in some cases not followed our rule about spelling of names and writing of XVII Dynasty in text and XVIII in footnotes.(36)

In December 1915, a letter to Winlock criticised lots of points particularly about American and English spellings and use of words. 'Shoved', he asked Winlock, '... is this right in America, in England the word is rather slangy'.(37) The same gruff and impatient tone was used towards others, even to Lythgoe. It was to a degree the style of the period, as the use of surnames indicate. On the other hand the relationship between the two men could be very relaxed and friendly, even with Herbert Winlock:.

> Dear Winlock, your letter was a corker, and we roared with laughter over your pictures of conditions at the Museum and elsewhere. Seriously though, Lythgoe has had a rotten time of it and I wonder he doesn't have a nervous breakdown.(38)

It was also Mace who proposed that the publication of *The Tomb of Senebtisi at Lisht* should be co-authored and that particular chapters should not be attributed to one or other; Winlock was delighted by Mace's kindness:

> I am grateful to you about the collaboration scheme and as you seem to really want to and as I should be proud ...(39)

As the European powers entrenched themselves, Mace remained in London. He continued to be paid half his salary at Lythgoe's insistence, a generous subsidy which bothered him greatly. By the summer of 1915, Mace was anxious to play a more active part in the war. He was, however, over forty:

> I have been trying for several weeks now to break into the army ... I am over the age limit for regular enlistment in the ranks ... I have been unsuccessful, but I think I shall get in eventually if I can pass my medical. One of my attempts was on the Bankers' Battalion of the New Army. I intend to subscribe myself managing director, cashier and office boy of the Lisht and Provincial Night and Day Bank!(40)

The letter, despite its humorous references to the Lisht Bank gives reason to believe that even at this date Arthur was concerned about his health. He

*War service 1914–1919.
This photograph was
probably taken in Italy.
(From the collection of
Margaret Orr)*

persisted, however, and in September, by lying about his age and claiming he
was thirty-nine, was enlisted in the 2nd Battalion, the 28th London Territorial
Regiment. As the Regiment tended to attract similar 'arty types' it was known
as 'the Artists' Rifles'. An excited note was sent to Lythgoe; 'Just a line to tell
you I've got in at last ... The medical was an embarrassment'.(41) The Artists'
Rifles was basically a regiment that Lord Kitchener turned into an Officer
Training Corps with men then going to all regiments. (It later became the 21st
S. A. S. Regiment.) Volunteering to train as an instructor in field engineering,
Mace was promoted to the rank of Sergeant. Meanwhile Winifred was
expecting a second child. This, plus his new army status prompted him to think
about what would happen if he were to be killed; there was some consolation in
knowing that the family would help:

> Fortunately I have the satisfaction of knowing that if I got scuppered the
> family would not starve, for Winifred's family would look after them.(42)

In the meantime he anguished about his current state of financial affairs and
refused to draw a salary, telling Lythgoe that Winifred's family were helping
out:

> Naturally I don't like accepting money from my father-in-law and I don't
> like eating into my small capital ... but ... it's war and we are all in the same
> boat ... worth it to put those damned Germans where they belong.(43)

Lythgoe's letters to Mace were full of attempts to persuade him to take his
salary and finding all sorts of face-saving ways to do it.

It was Mace's hope that he would be posted to Egypt where he believed
his Arabic would be useful. To his frustration this was not to be as his health
increasingly gave cause for concern. As a result he was transferred to the Army

Service Corps and served in England and Italy. His letters expressed frustration, as he wrote to Lythgoe on 7 November 1917, 'I am still dealing with food supplies and shunting trains ...' Before his demobilisation in 1919 he sent a postcard to the Metropolitan showing himself and his staff seated outside a supplies depot:

> This is just to show you how we brave the vigours of the Italian Campaign. You will see from our expressions how little attention we pay to bursting shells. We say let 'em burst and they do - three hundred miles away. In the background the delicatessen store of which I have the honour to be the manager. The brutal and licentious British Soldiery grouped around are my staff!(44)

*Postcard sent to New York towards the end of his military service in Italy. (From the collection of Margaret Orr)*

Anxious to hear about his colleagues he was always amused by any news of Lindsley Hall, thus on 7 November 1917, he asked Lythgoe, 'How about Hall, the daredevil desperado of the western prairie; itching to be in the thick of it I suppose'. To relieve his own boredom and frustration at not being in the thick of things there was always drawing and short stories to write. As his mother had once suggested, these were very useful gifts. Health continued to be a problem and letters home contain reports of bronchitis and malaria:

> I had a rotten time when I came out here first, living in a tent with deep snow all around and 29°C of frost ... consequently I developed one of my bouts of fever and had a couple of weeks in hospital.(45)

There must have been consolation and satisfaction in seeing the publication of *The Tomb of Senebtisi at Lisht* in 1916. The Museum announced the publication, 'of the discovery of the tomb of a noble lady who was buried at Lisht' as one of 'the most important which the Museum has issued'.(46) The Metropolitan was not alone in its belief, as the publication received a glowing review from Professor James H. Breasted, of the University of Chicago, which the Bulletin of the Metropolitan Museum of Art rather coyly reprinted in its November 1917 edition. The Bulletin's editor, in a footnote, said it was printing the Professor's review which had appeared originally in *The Nation*, 'because it says some things which the Museum could not say, but which it has justifiable pleasure in reading'. In *A Lady of the Nile* Breasted was fulsome in his praise, especially of the fieldwork:

> The fieldwork of this expedition has been conducted after the most rigid scientific methods, as they have been developed in recent years; and this volume shows that the discoveries made are to be reported in the same careful scientific spirit.(47)

Furthermore with its detailed records, observations and careful preservation, Senebtisi was a model of how field work should be done. He compared the excavation very favourably with the unsatisfactory recovery of 'the treasure of Dahshur'. It was Breasted's belief that the Metropolitan's vigorous department of Egyptian Art had managed to balance the need for recovering Egyptian Art for the benefit of the Museum's public with 'the requirements of archaeological science'. In terms of Mace and Winlock's findings, Breasted saw the publication as 'a compendium of the burial practices of the Middle Kingdom'. He was not always convinced about the conclusions reached, but believed the fault lay not in their treatment of particular problems, but that given the state of knowledge at the time these problems were insoluble. The burial of Senebtisi was important because it was the largely intact burial of a 'lady of rank'. In contrast, however, to the solid gold jewellery of the Dahshur princesses, Senebtisi's jewellery was often paste and gold leaf, and thus demonstrated the lesser resources of her position. It was also the case that Senebtisi's funerary equipment was remarkably simple compared to the type until then considered typical of the XII Dynasty: there were no model Nile boats, no estate models showing activities to continue in the afterlife, no elaborate object friezes painted on the coffin interior. Mace and Winlock believed that Senebtisi was a 'court type burial' and the other, in contrast, a 'provincial type'. They also saw a chronological distinction, with Senebtisi as the later type. Both distinctions remain important in the study of Egyptian Middle Kingdom burial practices, though the analysis has been refined and modified as more information and new studies become available. Senebtisi still serves, however, as an important, finely detailed record of a Middle Kingdom burial and a reference point for studies of the subject.

In England, Arthur's other Nile lady, Winifred, had closed up the house at St. John's Wood and with Margaret spent the war years with her family in Walsall or in a variety of rented houses in the south-east. A second daughter Anne was born with Down's Syndrome on 8 November 1915. In New York, Lythgoe was missing Arthur's company, as he wrote on 16 May 1918:

> This business has gone on so long that it seems ages since I watched you cutting off those (delicately thin) slices of cold ham for your breakfast, and later sprinting out over the sand hummocks in your canvas sneakers for that beloved pyramid of yours.(48)

With the war finally over at the end of 1918, Arthur was run down and unwell; 'I haven't had a real rest since I joined the army' he wrote. Illness and lack of energy made him irritable, 'the country seems upside down, but I suppose one can't expect anything else after such a big upheaval - but the folks of our class are having the worst of it'.(49) As he waited for demobilisation the ever thoughtful Lythgoe, conscious of the fact that Mace was in no fit state to go immediately back to fieldwork suggested he:

> ... come over here with your family and spend a year or so in New York getting this new material arranged and installed. The Lahun jewellery particularly has got to be thoroughly worked over and we've got several similar jobs which I know would be just to your liking including Theodore Davis Scarabs and the installation of a new room of jewellery and ornament in which you could be of the greatest help to us.

Furthermore, Lythgoe arranged to have a suitable salary and travelling arrangements made so that:

> ... the present high cost of living in New York will not be a burden to you.(50)

Arthur Mace's value as a member of the Department of Egyptian Art was evident and as Lythgoe suggested, he spent the 1919–1920 season in New York principally on the restoration of the two Lahun jewel caskets or toilet boxes which the Museum had purchased from Petrie. Petrie found the caskets in 1914 when he made an extensive search of the pyramid and cemetery of the XII Dynasty King Senwosret II at El Lahun and found the grave of his presumed Princess Sit-hathor-yunet. Although the grave had been disturbed and robbed, the intruders had missed the pair of ebony caskets with their jewellery and toilet articles. Unfortunately, despite avoiding plunder, they had not escaped the vicissitudes of almost forty centuries of rain and floods and had been reduced to thousands of fragments of ivory and gold. Removed to England, the fragments had been washed and sorted, and in the spring of 1916 they were purchased by

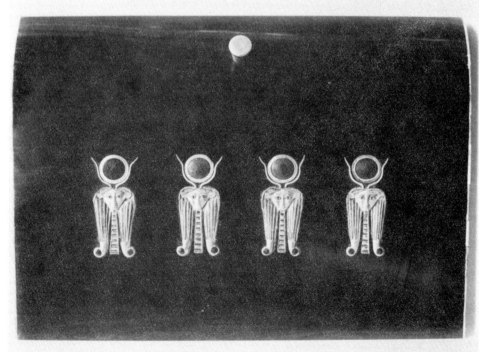

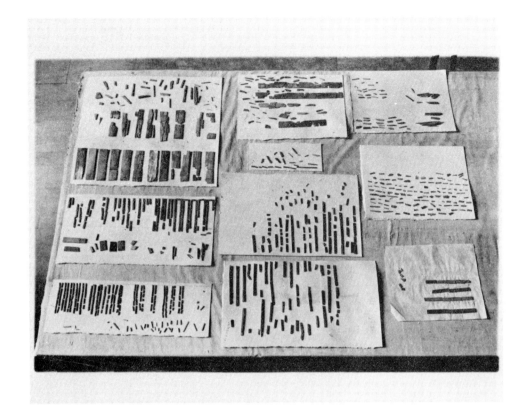

the Metropolitan although they were not shipped to New York until the autumn of 1919. Mace was ideally suited to taking charge of the restoration. The pieces were first soaked to remove damaging salts, then sorted by size and shape and finally glued. As much of the wood had already disintegrated it was necessary to use new wood. An existing box of the same period in the Louvre was used for reference and to some extent as Mace admitted the restoration was 'frankly conjectural'.(51) Nevertheless, the result was magnificent and Lythgoe was delighted:

> The Museum seems to have been rewarded with visitors all summer, many of them from other parts of the country. That jewellery room is the great drawing card and those caskets the centre of everything. You did a wonderful job and you'll never need any further monument! They seem more gorgeous now than ever.(52)

As Lythgoe was to say after Mace's death, the reconstruction of the two caskets were, 'one of the most elaborately painstaking and accurate pieces of archaeological reconstruction within my knowledge'.(53)

Towards the end of the winter of 1920, Mace delivered a lecture in the Museum on the theme of Egyptian Literature. Despite the difficulties of language involved in any such study he aimed through example to demonstrate the vitality of Egyptian poetry and prose. Egyptian poetry was, he emphasised, essentially lyric in character and depended on rhythm other than rhyme or

*Opposite: The larger of the Lahun caskets, as restored by Mace at the Metropolitan during the winter of 1919–1920.*

*Below: The lid of the above*

*This page: Fragments of the Lahun caskets prior to restoration.*

*(Courtesy of the Metropolitan Museum of Art, New York, acc. no. 16.1.1, ca. 1897–1797BC, Rogers Fund and Henry Walters Gift 1916)*

metre; nevertheless he found familiar themes of love and death in Egypt two-and-a-half thousand years before Christ. Attention was also drawn to the debt that later writers, particularly the Hebrews owed to the Egyptians. Themes of death and resurrection occur in both Egyptian poetry and prose. *The Hymns to Aton* supposed to have been written by the heretic King Akhenaten has so many similarities to *Psalm 104*, 'that it is hard to escape the conclusion that the writer of the latter must have known and been influenced by the hymn'.(54) Equally the semi-poetic *Song of the Harper* :

> ... Be joyful then;  rest not from merriment; for at the end none taketh ought away,
> And when he goes he cometh not again.

Its message of eat, drink and be merry for tomorrow we die, finds echoes 'in *Ecclesiastes*, in *Omar Khayyam*, and all down the ages'. Mace also pointed out that Egyptian folk tales were the oldest known and they were also the first to use many popular themes. Thus the story of Ali Baba and other tales of th*e Arabian Nights* used themes and plots known to the ancient Egyptians. The same could be said for Boccaccio's *Decameron* which used an old story of King Khufu and the magicians. There was as Mace said nothing new under the sun. This lecture on literature was later printed by the Metropolitan as a tribute to Mace.

From late 1920 until the spring of 1922, the expedition returned to Lisht and resumed their pre-war programme. The main aim of the first season's work would be the successful clearance of the western side of the pyramid. That Arthur Mace was still unwell is clear from his letters and by his increased tendency to be slightly irritable with his colleagues. As was often the case Lindsley Hall was the focus of his displeasure. He wrote for example to Winlock, in Thebes, on 19 September 1920; 'I rather hope Hall will be away there for a month or so for if I have his undiluted company all season I fear my brain will give way'. There were also occasions when he seemed to be rather exasperated by the problems of sharing workmen or resources with Winlock and the Theban branch of the work. At any rate, by mid-November he was in bed with fever. By the end of the month he had improved. Arthur was always happier when Winifred was with him, but with two small children, this became more difficult. A letter of 26 November 1920, noted their wedding anniversary:

> Do you know Darling, yesterday was our betrothal day, and I never said anything about it, and I thought of it some days ago, and meant to. Fourteen years ago since you put your hand in mine, and twenty one since I fell in love with you and developed photographs most of the night!

They clearly missed each other and one evening when Lindsley Hall was playing Winifred's piano, which had survived the war years, Mace wrote:

> ... and really it's in wonderful condition considering. The sound of it brought back so many memories, and made me want you so badly ...(55)

He betrayed all the classic symptoms of a man missing his family when he had tea with the Omdah and took photographs of his 'chicks', Margaret and Anne to

*Mace's field diary, for 1921, recording the important discovery of a foundation deposit at the south west corner of King Amenemhat I at Lisht. (Courtesy of the Egyptian Expedition, Metropolitan Museum of Art, New York)*

### 20 SUNDAY [51-314]
2 in Lent

Found Foundation Deposit at S.W corner
of Pyramid.
also 2 F.D's in corners of Funet Mast.

### 21 MONDAY [52-313]

Hall's friend Frazer out from Cairo.
Clean F.D.
Found in pit stone statuette on Offering Table.
Took up F.D. at SE corner of Funet Mast.

### 22 TUESDAY [53-312]

Took up F.D.
Containing ox-head, vases, saucers & small
buckets. These buckets contained tiles with
cartouche of Amenhat I, too coffer etc -
Took up F.D. at NW corner of Funet Mast.

### 23 WEDNESDAY [54-311]

Photographed F.D. at S.W corner of Funet Mast.
Frazer Go. to Cairo, & Hall with him
for one night.

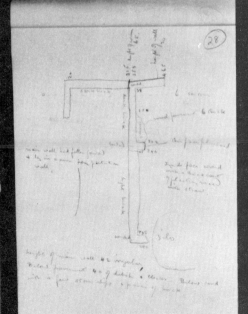

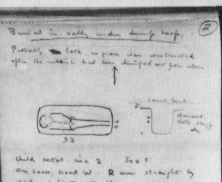

show him. There was consolation in the warmth he received from the villagers many of whom were old friends. He was amazed at how the boys had grown and how people treated him as if he were 'Squire of Lisht'.(56)

Work was always a good diversion for the homesick and preparations had to be made for the visit of the Museum's Director Dr. Edward Robinson and his wife. They clearly had a great deal of fun organising this and, as is so often the case with 'state visits', the event was stage-managed to give the best possible impression. Lythgoe received a full report of the visit which Mace reported tongue in cheek:

> Did I hear you say something about the dirty old boat? Not a bit of it. Abd el Ghani had risen to the occasion. On either bank of the canal there was an approach of clean white sand. The boat had been likewise scrubbed and strewn likewise with sand, and on the poop deck two chairs, I mean thrones - I'm sure Mrs. Robinson felt like Cleopatra on her barge.(57)

Lythgoe hoped Mace would find the tombs of the Princesses of Amenemhat I and that a comparable treasure to that found at Lahun would be their reward. In the event Mace did find the burial shafts, but they were empty.(58) Even the coffins had been removed; the only object of note to be found was a single heavy gold bracelet. Of great importance, however, was the discovery of one of the pyramid foundation deposits in the south west corner. The hole contained an ox skull, six roughly shaped bricks of clay, and a mass of broken pottery. The bricks were found to contain plaques inscribed with the name of King Amenemhat I, confirmation of the pyramid's inhabitant. Mace was very excited by the find and told Winifred in a letter of 22 February 1921; 'It's rather an important find, because pyramid foundation deposits are extremely rare'. The find coincided with Margaret's eighth birthday which prompted Arthur to think of the night she was born:

> This night eight years ago darling, was I suppose the most anxious one I ever spent. It seemed as if it would last for ever. It certainly must have been the worst that you ever went through, but it was worth it, wasn't it? What a difference it made to our lives, and what a lovely time it was afterwards. Truly she was a child of joy and I am sure that this influenced her character.(59)

Arthur also recalled his own eighth birthday:

> I spent it at Woodsden (Tasmania) and in a piece of bread at breakfast were five sovereigns ... just over a year afterwards we sailed for England.(60)

Sometimes there was, as he wrote of his children, sadness, particularly given Anne's condition. Thus he said, 'They're darlings, both of them, and I wish we had twice as many, but maybe it's wiser not'.(61)

Mace was finding the work, particularly with the foundation deposit, very interesting, but there was an air of weariness about him. Perhaps it was time for a change or at least for writing up and consolidating the work so far. He was beginning to feel that as far as the Museum was concerned the effort and the cost expended were becoming too great for the results provided. The department was also supporting Winlock's large scale excavations in Luxor. With all this in mind he told Lythgoe:

> I shan't be sorry to get through with it, for to tell you the truth I'm beginning to get a bit weary of that infernal old pyramid.(62)

In February 1922, Mace cabled Lythgoe for further funding, 'To finish pyramid satisfactorily would need four to five hundred pounds'.(63) Winlock also required more money for his work at Thebes. Lythgoe decided that Mace should stop work immediately at Lisht and that their scarce funds should go to Winlock. The following season, he proposed, should be used by Mace to begin work at home on the publication of the North Pyramid. Ambrose Lansing would then complete the work at Lisht. Always concerned about his staff, Lythgoe tried to put Mace's mind at ease and told him not to worry about the lack of finds. Mace was understanding, but confessed to being rather taken aback by the decision. He told Lythgoe that there was about a month's further work to be done and he would rather do it himself than let Lansing do it as it would be '... impossible to explain to him just what I'm after ...'.(64) That Arthur was anxious about the situation can be judged from the fact that he had written to Winifred as soon as he had Lythgoe's cable expressing his concern that Lansing 'might make the big find of the whole season'.(65) Lythgoe was obviously persuaded that Mace should return for one more year as a letter of 10 March 1922, indicated. Lythgoe had also decided that Mace would be more organised for writing up his notes either in England or New York. This then was the plan until the autumn, when proposed changes in the Antiquities law, indicated that the customary division of objects, (half and half, between the excavators and the Egyptians) was to be tightened up in the Egyptians' favour. Lythgoe naturally felt that to justify the expense of the year's excavations he had to direct the department's energies to the most promising site and 'get all the stuff we can while we can insist on a full half'.(66) Winlock seemed keen to have Mace work alongside him and had told Lythgoe that the hill at Thebes, with its XI Dynasty tombs, appealed to Mace and would be the most likely site for notable finds.(67) Later on in the season Mace could resume work at Lisht and make his hoped for find. As he wrote in his report, 'There are certain aspects of a digger's life which may well be described like second marriages, as the triumph of hope over experience', or as he put it more succinctly to Winifred, 'who'd be a digger'.(68)

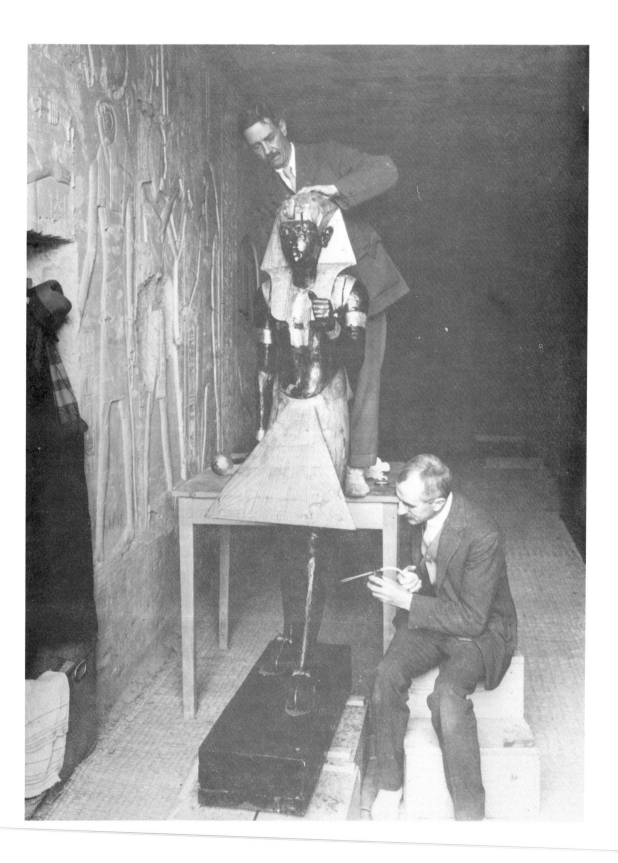

CHAPTER FOUR

# 'It takes
# one's breath away'

with Carnarvon, Howard Carter
and the tomb of Tutankhamun

In the autumn of 1922 a somewhat dispirited Arthur Mace made preparations to depart for Egypt and the Metropolitan's second Theban dig. The sudden discovery of the magnificent tomb of Tutankhamun in November by Howard Carter was to present Mace with the kind of opportunity most Egyptologists only dream about. The contribution of Mace and his colleagues in the clearing, recording and conservation of artefacts was of major significance. It was estimated by Howard Carter that had it not been for the on-site conservation work for which Mace had responsibility then barely ten per cent of the material would have been in a fit state for exhibition when it reached Cairo.(1) Mace's contribution has perhaps been appreciated by some of those working in the field but, for public consumption the lions' share of attention has always been directed at Howard Carter and his aristocratic patron Lord Carnarvon. Mace was partly to blame - he shunned publicity - but in the embattled decade that followed the discovery, little attention was given to ensure that the name of this early, important colleague was not forgotten, particularly after his death in 1928.

The story of the search and discovery of the tomb of Tutankhamun is too well-known and well-documented elsewhere to require repeating in detail.(2) Briefly, however, it was on 4 November 1922, that one of Carter's workmen discovered the top step of a flight of stairs in the Valley of the Kings which led to the tomb of Tutankhamun. With financial help from the Earl of Carnarvon,

*Mace (standing) and Lucas at work conserving one of the two guardian figures from the tomb of Tutankhamun. (Courtesy of the Griffith Institute, Oxford)*

Carter had been working for years in the hope of a major find in the valley. They were on the verge of giving up, but Carter's persistence paid off and he was able to cable his patron, George Edward Stanhope Molyneux Herbert, Fifth Earl of Carnarvon:

> At last have made wonderful discovery in Valley; a magnificent tomb with seals intact; recovered same for your arrival; congratulations.(3)

Lord Carnarvon sailed at once for Egypt and late on the afternoon of 26 November, with his daughter Lady Evelyn Herbert, he watched Carter break through the sealed door, at the bottom of a passageway leading from the steps. Carter later recorded what he had seen:

> At first I could see nothing, the hot air escaping from the chamber causing the candle flame to flicker but presently, as my eyes grew accustomed to the light, details of the room within emerged slowly from the mist, strange animals statues, and gold - everywhere the glint of gold.(4)

They immediately realised the significance of the find, which was to prove to be the most intact royal burial yet found. The world was electrified by the news and the press developed an insatiable appetite for the details of anything and everything connected with the tomb of the long dead pharaoh. Mace later tried to account for the interest:

> The explanation is, I suppose, simple enough really. It lies in the fact that we are all, even the most prosaic of us, children under our skins, and thrill deliciously at the very idea of buried treasure, sealed doorways, jewelled robes, inlay of precious stones, kings' regalia; the phrases grip, and we can now under care of scientific interest, openly and unashamedly indulge an intellectual appetite that has hitherto been nourished surreptitiously on detective stories and murder cases in the press.(5)

If Carter realised the significance of his discovery, he also understood the enormity of the task that faced him. Despite the financial backing of Lord Carnarvon he was an independent archaeologist working without the resources of a large institution. Fortunately, help in the form of the Metropolitan Museum of Art was at hand. On hearing of the discovery, Lythgoe immediately sent a telegram to Howard Carter with his congratulations and the offer of assistance. Carter was delighted and replied:

> Thanks message. Discovery colossal and needs every assistance. Could you consider loan of Burton in recording in time being? Costs to us. Immediate reply would oblige. Every regards, Carter.(6)

The Metropolitan's photographer Harry Burton (1879–1940) had a first class reputation for the quality of his archaeological photographs and Carter was anxious to secure his assistance.(7) Albert Lythgoe was himself an enthusiastic photographer and appreciated its importance. After discussions with his Director Edward Robinson he agreed to Carter's request and replied:

Only too delighted to assist in every possible way. Please call upon Burton and any other members of our staff. Am cabling Burton to that effect.(8)

With the expanded Theban dig not yet underway, Lythgoe was also in a position to add:

Now as to suggestions I would make as to the manner of our co-operation and assistance. Mace leaves for Trieste tomorrow and will be there at Thebes almost as soon as this letter. I have talked the whole matter over with him and I would suggest that you take him over bodily to assist. I know of no-one without exception, to compare with him in the patient and painstaking skill necessary for the preservation of evidence and fragile material such as you have apparently in your present 'find'. His latest piece of work for us in the case of those ivory caskets from Lahun was simply beyond all praise.(9)

Lythgoe also managed to convince Carnarvon that Mace was vital, as he told Robinson:

... Carnarvon realises now that Mace is the key to the whole situation and that he is without a rival in the patience and painstaking skill necessary in such an emergency as the present one. It is a case of Senebtisi multiplied to the nth degree.(10)

In addition Lythgoe offered the services of his draughtsmen, Lindsley Hall and Walter Hauser. Hauser (1893–1959) was an architect who had been with the Metropolitan since 1919.

Lythgoe's apparent selfless haste to send a large section of his department's staff to work for the notoriously difficult Carter has given rise to questions about his motivations. It was, however, the case that the Metropolitan and Howard Carter were well acquainted: since 1910 they had excavated alongside each other at Thebes, where they had shared information and ideas. The Metropolitan, like the British Museum, had obtained some important antiquities from the art market through Carter's agency. They had also received many gifts from Lord Carnarvon and were anxious 'to repay those many kindnesses'.(11) With the prospect of a rather dull season ahead and the knowledge that Mace required a stimulating project, to boost his flagging morale, Lythgoe was as anxious as everyone else to become involved in the great discovery, and 'assist in every way in the preservation for posterity of the remarkable material and evidence contained in the tomb'.(12) As Mace had not yet begun his work at Thebes it would also be easy for Lythgoe to divert him to help Carter. Lythgoe knew of course that helping Carter and Carnarvon might also benefit the museum in terms of objects not required by Cairo Museum, as had been the practice. He also felt that anything the Metropolitan might get in return from Tutankhamun would balance Mace's redirection away from the XI Dynasty tombs. For Lythgoe the benefits of cooperation on such a project were clear and he knew Mace with Carter would ensure the Metropolitan's involvement was worthy.(13)

Arthur Mace travelled to Luxor by train on Christmas Eve, 1922. It was,

*The Metropolitan House at Deir el Bahri. (Courtesy of the Metropolitan Museum of Art, New York)*

as he told Winifred in a letter written on Boxing Day, a very comfortable journey, 'with a compartment to myself and a Christmas Eve Dinner in the train with turkey, plum pudding and rum punch'.(14) His home for the next few months was to be with Helen and Herbert Winlock in the Metropolitan's dig house on the left bank of the Nile opposite Luxor. Metropolitan House (often known in Britain as the American house, but one has to consider Chicago House founded a few years later), was a rather palatial mud brick affair which had been built in 1912 for those working on the Asasif, as Winlock's concession was known. The cost of construction had been authorised by the museum's President J. P. Morgan, who was 'of the opinion that the quality of the work was never improved by uncomfortable living and so the Museum staff were to live simply but well'.(15) Mace was to find it a far cry from Petrie's camp and even from the relative comfort of Lisht. The building constructed in the Coptic style was designed by Winlock and Walter Jones and was influenced by their archaeological work at such sites, with its rather grand public rooms and what Mace described as its 'social whirl', and 'none could feel that they had been slumming or boast they had roughed it'.(16) In these rather elegant surroundings there was Christmas Dinner with all the trimmings. In the dining room that evening were Mace, Herbert Winlock (Helen was ill in bed), Norman and Nina de Garis Davies, Wilkinson, Lindsley Hall, Walter Hauser, Howard Carter and Alfred Lucas. Alfred Lucas (1867–1945), a Manchester born chemist who worked in Cairo for the Egyptian government, had volunteered to give up his holidays to help Carter. He and Arthur were to work closely together. The Christmas festivities were completed with crackers and paper hats. Mace was amused to see that poor Lindsley Hall's was 'appropriately a granny cap'.

In contrast to the previous season's letters home to Winifred, the correspondence from Luxor was full of Arthur's excitement about the prospect of the work ahead. As he wrote:

> Here I am in the thick of it. I lunched with Carter today and am to start in on the tomb tomorrow. It is a simply stupendous thing, so much so that it takes ones breath away and leaves one reeling.(17)

By all accounts Carter made Mace warmly welcome:

> Carter was extremely friendly, and seems to take for granted that I am assigned to the job for the duration, which might mean two or three seasons in the field to say nothing of further work on restoration and publication.(18)

They had met several times in the past and Carter had been very hospitable when Mace made his first visit to the valley some years before. They had in common their experiences with Petrie and were bonded by their mutual meticulous attention to detail. In background and temperament they differed. Carter lacked the assurance which Mace's solid upper-middle class background and public school education had given him. Mace was steady and unassuming and inclined to introspection, Carter was irascible, outspoken and enjoyed the

*Mace (right) looks preoccupied while Carter poses for this formal photograph with Lord Carnarvon and his daughter Lady Evelyn Herbert. (Courtesy of The Times)*

*Arthur Mace, standing behind Harry Burton, outside the laboratory tomb of Seti II. (Courtesy of The Times)*

limelight. Their different characters were obvious from their appearance. The once dapper Mace now dressed for work with the lack of attention that goes with confidence and maturity. In his old Norfolk jacket and white sneakers he might have been mistaken for a head gardener. Carter on the other hand with his fastidious sense of dress, his bow ties, cigarette holder and gentlemanly accoutrements had the appearance of trying too hard. He betrayed his unease and lack of confidence. Perhaps, had the two men been more similar they would not have got on so well: as it was they established an ideal working partnership which was mutually beneficial.

It was agreed that Mace would be in charge of the on-site restoration of the objects as they were brought from the tomb. His work was therefore mainly in 'the laboratory'. In fact the laboratory was a makeshift affair established with the consent of the Antiquities Service in the narrow tomb of Seti II situated in a secluded spot a little way from the tomb of Tutankhamun. Hopefully he could work here with Lucas, away from the reporters who 'jump about like mad men with cameras'.(19) Objects were carried in procession from the tomb to the laboratory secured with cotton wool and bandages. Each box or stretcher of objects was examined in turn. First the surface dust was removed, using a feather duster or with very fragile textiles, blown off with the aid of hand bellows. Measurements were taken, archaeological notes written and copies of inscriptions made on large filing cards. This was followed by the appropriate conservation methods and photography, and a note of the techniques used made on the file card. In most cases 'no attempt at final treatment was made ... all we could do was to apply preliminary treatment, sufficient in any event to enable the object to support a journey in safety'.(20) He found the work fascinating and got 'a lot of valuable information as to the preservation of antiquities from Lucas'. As one writer pointed out, Mace was already 'thought by those in the profession to be a genius in conservation ...'(21)

The work was difficult and painstaking. As the tomb had been disturbed in antiquity, many of the contents had been hastily put back in a jumbled state when the attempted robbery was discovered. Thus caskets and boxes, which were themselves precious items requiring attention, were found to contain jewellery and textiles in the most fragile condition. During the early part of January, 1923, Mace spent a lot of time on a painted wooden box with a gesso coating; this was box number twenty-one in the register of objects. It appeared at first to be in remarkable condition and having removed the surface dust, 'the discolouration of the painted surfaces was reduced with benzine and the whole exterior of the caskets were sprayed with a solution of cellulose in amylacetate to fix the gesso to the wood ...'. All appeared to be well for three or four weeks,

*Alfred Lucas at work in the tomb laboratory of Seti II. (Courtesy of The Times)*

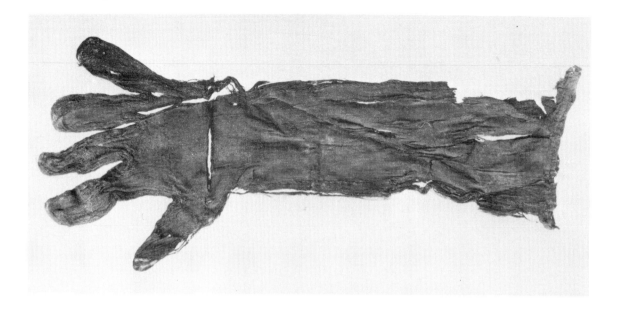

but the change in temperature from the tomb to the laboratory caused the wood to shrink, and the gesso to come away taking the painted surface with it. 'The position was serious', and Mace and Lucas decided to experiment with melted paraffin wax which proved to be ideal: it held the structure firmly and enhanced the colouration.(22) Inside the box were bead garments and sandals; there were also more problems, as he told Winifred:

> We have some fearful problems at the tomb. Just now we are working on a
> box which contains garments and shoes all covered with bead work. The
> cloth is so rotten you can hardly touch it, and the beads drop off the shoes if
> you look at them. Moreover resin has now run out and glued all the shoes
> together, so you can imagine what a job it is.(23)

It took him three weeks to work his way through this box. As he removed each layer he came upon: rush sandals, a gilt head rest, a beaded robe, leather sandals, slippers, and a mass of decayed and tangled cloth covered in spangles of rosettes and sequins of gold and silver. He also found a number of gloves.(24)

The gloves, those of a child, were to lead the archaeologists, painfully short of historical evidence about the reign of Tutankhamun, to some important conclusions. As Arthur told Winifred:

> I made a strange find among the king's robes today - a child's glove of cloth,
> belonging to a child I should say three or four years old. I imagine it must
> have been one of his own ...(25)

It gradually became clear that Tutankhamun came to the throne as a child and was possibly only in his late teens when he died. In a further letter he asked Winifred for some practical help with the glove:

*The cloth glove belonging to Tutankhamun which so intrigued Mace. (Courtesy of the Griffith Institute, Oxford)*

*In a letter to Winifred, Arthur records his discovery of the cloth glove. (From the collection of Margaret Orr)*

Luxor
Jan. 21st 1923

Dearest Wife,

I made a strange find among the King's robes today — a child's glove of cloth, belonging to a child I should say three or four years old. I imagine it must have been one of his own, as the inscription giving contents of another box said "The King's sidelock when a boy". I'm for that box emptied now thank goodness, and all it's contents sorted out and most of them noted. In a day or two I shall be able to get on to something else. By the way don't pass on any news to anyone else that I give you in letters, any details I mean about particular objects — general information of course does'nt matter. Tomorrow morning, Lucas and I are going to spend in the tomb itself, treating some of the things before they are moved. Carter asked me today if I should be willing to carry on with the work until it was finished. I told him I should as far as I was concerned, but did'nt know what New York would have to say about it, as it will probably mean two more seasons work before the tomb is finally cleared. I had a good look in to the second chamber today, and it is absolutely chock a block with fine things.

Jan. 22nd Spent the whole day in the tomb, treating the great bedsteads with wax. Then this afternoon we took one of them to pieces, and an anxious job it was. It had been too big to be taken into the tomb whole, so had been put together in the tomb itself. There are

By the way, could you take one of Margaret's ordinary tight fitting cotton gloves and measure the length of the biggest finger for me - from tip to where the other fingers branch off. I want to get the exact age of the child who wore my glove.(26)

The glove caused quite a sensation; Mace wrote a newspaper article on the subject and Dents the glove makers asked Carnarvon if they might have a photograph.(27) Other garments in the tomb led Mace to the same conclusions, especially as many were stamped with the King's cartouche. He noted his thoughts in his field diary entry for 5 February; 'Was Tutankhamun only a boy when he came to the throne?'(28)

The investigation of the box and its treatment was repeated over and over again during the next few months. From time to time there were visits to the tomb to provide remedial treatment for objects *in situ* or to escort them to the laboratory. Often the objects came from the tomb faster than Mace and Lucas could deal with them. Nevertheless, Mace applied his painstaking attention to them all. In the first few weeks he dealt with a wide range of objects including footstools, collars, pendants and statues. The most complex piece was a corslet which, broken and scattered, required extensive reconstruction and although depicted on monuments, it was the first time they had been 'lucky enough to find a complete example'. It was:

*The chariots before removal from the tomb. (Courtesy of The Times)*

*Mace and Lucas restore one of the King's chariots. (Courtesy of the Griffith Institute, Oxford)*

> ... a very elaborate affair, consisting of four separate parts - the corslet proper inlaid with gold and carnelian, with border bands and braces of gold and covered inlay: a collar with conventional imitation of beads in carnelian, and green and blue-faience; and two magnificent pectorals of openwork gold with covered inlay, one for the chest, the other to hang behind as make weight.(29)

Despite his long experience Mace was evidently moved by the quality and beauty of the objects. He can even be found using adjectives which he tended to avoid and disliked the excessive use of by others; thus he wrote to Winifred of 'a perfectly exquisite statuette of the King in dark blue glass' and such 'wonderful beadwork'.(30) The scale of the work involved can be judged from Mace's comments on one of the King's robes which, while the fabric was almost reduced to powder, was covered in an estimated fifty thousand beads. For those who might question the validity of the restoration work Mace wrote:

> These restorations are not only legitimate but absolutely essential to a proper appreciation and study of the material. By their means you acquire complete objects, things of beauty in themselves and of enormous archaeological value; without restorations you would have gained nothing but a large boxful of beads, a few pieces of ill-preserved cloth and a number of meaningless shells of gold decoration, things of but small archaeological value and from an artistic point of view no value at all.(31)

In early 1923, all seemed to be progressing well and Lythgoe felt able to write to Edward Robinson:

Our men are doing a magnificent piece of work and this whole procedure is running with clocklike regularity. Burton is the only one, who with his past experience behind him, could have possibly made such a marvellous fine record for all time by photography. Mace's careful and painstaking methods are producing an unparalleled series of notes and records, minute in every detail, while Hauser's and Hall's drawings and plans, giving the positions of the objects round out the completeness of the record to the nth degree.(32)

Mace told his wife that American visitors to the tomb were pleased to see the part their Museum was playing in the excavation. One called Morton Howell, the American Minister to Egypt, greeted Mace, 'Well, you boys of the New York Museum are doing wonderful work here in the valley, and we're going to let the world know about it'.(33) He knew the remark was kindly meant, but at this stage felt the help they were giving Carter and Carnarvon should remain a low key affair and was astute enough to know the dangers of excessive praise. Carter was a very independent man and would not have welcomed the world knowing the extent to which his operation depended on his American colleagues.

Other sensibilities which required careful handling were those of Herbert Winlock. For twelve years Winlock had been the significant figure in the Metropolitan's Theban excavations and now he had to operate alongside the more glamorous Tutankhamun excavation which involved his colleagues and deprived him of the undiluted assistance of Burton and Hauser. In February Arthur was able to tell Winifred that 'so far relations in our camp are excellent, though Winlock is a bit grouchy sometimes'. The following month he was more direct about Winlock's situation, 'Winlock has felt rather out of it about the tomb and also has rather felt his nose out of joint by Lythgoe's being there where he has reigned supreme for so many years'.(34) It has to be said that such

*Herbert Winlock's excavations at Thebes. (Courtesy of the Metropolitan Museum of Art, New York)*

*The journey to work. Left to right: Lucas, Callender, Carter and Mace. (From the collection of Margaret Orr)*

feelings are not unusual in the Museum world: archaeologists and curators are not above the jealousies that affect the rest of us! In his defence, Winlock was a highly-skilled archaeologist, perhaps right to feel aggrieved at his work being disrupted. Also at this time both his wife Helen and his daughter Frances who were with him, were ill. Family illness also cast a shadow over Arthur's life during 1923. It had been expected that Winifred would join him in the new year and she even had her passage to Alexandria booked with Thomas Cook. Margaret and Anne, however, seem to have gone through a phase of catching one childhood ailment after another and so chicken-pox, measles and influenza combined to make 1922–23 a gloomy winter for Winifred alone with the girls. Arthur was very disappointed:

> It's funny, but before your last letter came I didn't seem to be able to realise that you were coming and now I don't seem to realise that you are not.(35)

Arthur had hoped that as in the past Winifred would help him with the bead work and, like so many clever shy men, the presence of his wife seems to have given him a greater degree of security and confidence. Winifred was a very strong character and Arthur will have relied on her encouragement and advice particularly where the social side of the camp life was concerned. When Arthur was away Winifred spent a lot of time at her mother's in Walsall. This of course pleased Granny Blyth who was always happy to have company in the house she never left. Mrs. Blyth also worried, not unreasonably, about Arthur being in the 'bad air of the tomb'. Arthur tried to calm her fears telling Winifred that she needn't be alarmed 'because I'm hardly ever in it, I am nearly all the time in our workshop tomb, which is

beautifully fresh and airy'.(36) In early spring the sorry tale of family health problems continued and Margaret had to undergo an operation for appendicitis. These anxieties, when so far from home, were the last thing he needed, given that the Tutankhamun material required such concentration and application and that he was already under a degree of stress. There was guilt too: Winifred had to take the decision for Margaret's operation alone; 'you poor darling, it must have been awful for you having to make the decision by yourself, but you were very wise and I can never thank you enough'.(37)

The working day was long, beginning with a donkey ride from Metropolitan House to the Valley of the Kings, accompanied by camels taking supplies to the tombs. The time spent travelling to and from the tomb was cut when Carter managed to acquire a Ford car; as Arthur reported, 'We are very swell now we go to work by car'.(38) There was usually a break for lunch. Just as there was a tomb for a laboratory, so there was a luncheon tomb, and Mace sat down to a formally laid, white covered, dining table with Carter, Burton, Callender and any visitors to the site. Arthur R. Callender (Pecky) was a friend of Carter's; Arthur told Winifred that he was 'a decent sort, but a bit rough'. He was an architect and engineer who had worked with Egyptian railways and retired to run a farm at Esneh. His skills were very useful and he could handle Carter. Less able to cope with Carter's moods were Hauser and Hall, and following a row in early February Mace feared they would refuse to work in the tomb.(39)

Mace seemed to have had little problem in working with Carter. Their roles were complementary and with Mace in the laboratory and Carter in the

*The journey to and from the tomb was shortened when Carter acquired a car. Carter is seen with the driver and seated, left to right, in the rear are Mace, Burton and Lucas. (From the collection of Margaret Orr)*

tomb they did not get under one anothers' feet. By applying himself to the tasks in hand, eschewing intrigue and quietly and calmly offering advice and guidance, Mace was of the greatest value to Carter. At the same time Mace was in a position to observe Carter and Carnarvon from the side-lines, to provide the necessary technical advice when it was called for and to act as a restraint on Carter's impulsive nature. He realised that Carter was a complex man or as he told Winifred: 'Carter is a queer chap, and gets very nervy sometimes from the responsibility - I don't wonder, but he's always very nice to me'.(40) By the end of January they were getting on very well and:

> Carter asked me today if I should be willing to carry on with the work until it was finished. I told him I should as far as I was concerned, but didn't know what New York would have to say about it ...(41)

By April, Carter was including Mace in his plans for publications and lectures:

> He was most generous in his ideas that I should kind of come into partnership with the firm and share in all the benefits that accrue therefrom. He also wanted to know if I would share a kind of lecturing programme with him. I don't know what to think.(42)

The indecision about Carter's offer probably reflected Mace's concern about the volatile side of Carter's character and the prospect of being too closely involved with him. He also had serious doubts about Carter's ability as a lecturer, as he told his mother-in-law in a letter of 16 April:

*Luncheon is served in a tomb, with Callender at the head of the table with Mace, Carter and Dr. Gardiner on the right and Lucas, Burton and Breasted on the left. (From the collection of Margaret Orr)*

> The question of lectures is going to be rather a serious one. I don't think
> Carter has ever given one in his life, and he doesn't in the least know how
> to set about it.(43)

In fact Mace's fears about Carter's abilities as a lecturer were unfounded. He
was to prove, as H. V. F. Winstone illustrates, an effective public speaker and
his lectures were a tremendous success.(44) At night, after dinner, the two men
began to collaborate on the first publication about the tomb:

> He and I are trying to get a small popular book written to hand in to the
> publishers when we get home. I've done the first chapter and most of the
> second, and today he was dictating to me his actual account of the discovery
> of the tomb. I think it should make an interesting little book with plenty of
> illustrations and if we get it out quick enough, ought to sell like anything.(45)

Carter and Mace did indeed manage to produce a bestseller and the book still
ranks as the most popular archaeological account ever written. Volume One and
part of Volume Two bear the the stamp of Mace. An original draft of the major
part of the book is in Mace's handwriting. In recent years the book has been
printed with Mace's name notably absent from the cover.

As well as writing for the book there were articles for the press. These
were designed to provide the world with information in a factual rather than
sensational way and at the same time retain public interest. In one article for *The
Times*, 'Dispatch number 5', Mace attempted to give his readers an idea about
the real work of an excavator and to explain why they worked so slowly and
carefully:

> Carelessness is criminal. Mistakes are irreparable. A single hasty ill considered
> action may be sufficient to damage, or even completely destroy, an object
> which a knowledge of the exact preservative required would have rendered
> safe for all time: or may result again in the irrevocable loss of information
> which the present may well be the only chance to secure.(46)

A further piece in *The Times* by Mace was used in March to justify the decision
to exclude tourists from the tomb and laboratory. The public's attention was
drawn to the dangers posed by a constant stream of visitors to the objects.
'Movements of strangers', he wrote 'in this narrow space add considerably to
the risks of minor accidents, such as the joining of a delicate object, or the
passing sweep of a skirt over a precarious gold leaf surface, are bound to occur'.
He also pointed out the dangers of atmospheric change and how half-an-hour
spent with a visitor could be half-an-hour lost in the treatment of an object. His
article was not only an impassioned justification for excluding the public but
also provided them with a graphic description of the work of an increasingly
scientific profession with its many duties:

*The handwritten original manuscript of ten chapters by Arthur Mace for 'The Tomb of Tutankhamun'. (From the collection of Margaret Orr)*

> And they are duties. Let there be no misapprehension about that. We owe it
> to the past no less than to the future to deal conscientiously with the
> wonderful wealth of material to which we have fallen heirs, and we have no
> right to jeopardise our chances of making the fullest possible use of it in order

Chapter 1

The King and the Queen

A few preliminary words about Tutankhamen, though
probably at the present moment he needs an introduction less
than anyone in History. He was the son in law, as everyone knows,
of that most written about, and probably most over rated, of all the
Egyptian Pharaohs, the heretic king Akhnaton. Of his parentage
we know nothing. He may have been of the blood royal and
had some indirect claim on the throne on his own account. He
may on the other hand have been a mere commoner. The point is
immaterial, for, by his marriage to a king's daughter, he at
once, by Egyptian law of succession, became a potential heir
to the throne. A hazardous and uncomfortable position it
must have been to fill at this particular stage of the history.
Consider the position situation, abroad, the empire founded
by Thothmes III, and held, with difficulty it is true, but
still held, by succeeding monarchs had crumpled up like a
pricked balloon; At home dissatisfaction was rife. The
priests of the ancient faith, who had seen their gods flouted
and their very livelihood compromised, were straining at
the leash, and only waiting the psychological moment to
slip it altogether; the soldier class, condemned to a
mortified inaction, were seething with discontent, and
apt for any form of excitement; the foreign mercenary element,
introduced in such large numbers since the wars of
conquest, were now, at a time of weakness, a sure and
certain focus of intrigue; the merchants peoples the
manufacturers and traders, as foreign trade declined
and home credit was divorced to a local and
ever narrowing circumscribed area, were rapidly becoming sullen
and discontented; the common populace, intolerant of
change, grieving, mass of them, at the loss of their old
familiar gods, and ready enough to attribute any loss,
deprivation, or misfortune they sustained to the jealous intervention

*Outside the laboratory tomb with, left to right, Callender, Carter and Mace. (Courtesy of The Times)*

*An unusually relaxed moment outside the tomb of Tutankhamun with Mace (second from left) standing between Lord Carnarvon and Carter. (Courtesy of The Times)*

to satisfy the claims of idle or even intelligent curiosity.(47)

If the press had its uses, as a means of disseminating information it also had its drawbacks. To begin with it meant the presence of large numbers of journalists and photographers who got in the way. Their reports to their readers at home encouraged those with the means to make their way to the Valley of the Kings. Egypt had long been on the itinerary of wealthy Europeans and Americans and Tutankhamun confirmed the exotic call of the east. Reporters seemed to be lurking behind every rock. As Arthur Mace wrote, 'Haven't the newspapers gone crazy? I don't see the *Daily Mail* accounts, but the *Morning Post* ones are bad enough'.(48) As a means of coping with the press Lord Carnarvon came to an arrangement with *The Times*. It alone would report on the excavation which was already operating in a less than favourable political climate. Frustrated reporters from other newspapers were furious about the embargo they suddenly faced. The Egyptian press were outraged at having to rely on hand-outs from *The Times*, to report on an excavation in their own country. Even Arthur found himself having to tell Winifred, 'don't pass on any news to anyone else that I give you in letters'.(49) Further references to Winifred about *The Times* arrangement showed Arthur's concern and his understanding of the reaction it promoted. On 23 January 1923, he wrote that the whole newspaper world was 'agog about our arrangements with *The Times* news service and all sorts of things are threatened ... it's a funny business on the whole this', and a few days later, 'Things have got rather lively the last few days owing to Lord Carnarvon's agreement with *The Times* which is much more drastic now we have seen it. It has caused a perfect storm'.(50) Mace believed Carnarvon was acting on the best of motives, but that he plunged into things without thinking. He began to be irritated by Carnarvon, 'He potters around all day, and will talk and ask questions and waste one's time'.

Unwittingly, Lord Carnarvon had brought together the ingredients for mischief making. This was particularly the case during a heightened period of Egyptian Nationalism. The excluded journalists had the opportunity and excuse to make trouble. One particularly difficult personality who seems to have been disliked by the majority of Carter's team was Arthur Weigall, a former Antiquities Service Inspector who had been appointed by the *Daily Mail* as their special correspondent. Mace realised that Weigall 'was going to have a rather uncomfortable time' and anyway found it difficult himself to be cordial to this man and described his reports as yarns.(51) It would be wrong to picture the valley as a refuge of poisonous hacks; many of those sent to report on the find were distinguished and respected writers like H. V. Morton the travel writer who represented *The Daily Express*. He found himself in an uncompromising position in Luxor waging 'a bitter campaign on behalf of the Egyptians ...'(52) It was to Morton that Weigall commented on Carnarvon's rather excitable mood when he first visited the tomb: 'If he goes down in that spirit I give him six weeks to live.' At the time these were light-hearted comments, but they turned out to be strangely prophetic. It is little wonder that Margaret Mace is convinced that the curse of Tutankhamun had little to do with the wrath of a boy king dead more than three thousand years and rather more to do with a group of disaffected journalists.(53) Inevitably, Luxor became a 'hotbed of gossip and intrigue'. Arthur described the situation:

The Winter Palace is a scream. None talks of anything but the tomb, newspaper men swarm, and you daren't say a word without looking round everywhere to see if anyone is listening. Some of them are trying to make mischief between Carnarvon and the Department of Antiquities, and all Luxor takes sides one way or another. Archaeology plus journalism is bad enough, but when you add politics it becomes a little too much.(54)

Mace was able to remain detached and perhaps rather smugly told Winifred; 'I steer beautifully out of it all' and 'However, it's amusing I can hold my tongue with anyone ...'(55) For others the situation was uncomfortable and it created tensions; Carter who carried the whole weight and responsibility for the situation became quite irritable with Lord Carnarvon. Mace was amazed to hear Carter talking to him 'like a naughty child' and observed how strained their relationship was becoming. At one point he felt sure that 'Carter's nerves are giving out with all the worry, and he'll have a breakdown if he isn't careful'.(56)

The tension was of course not just about newspaper coverage; as Mace reported there was a liberal sprinkling of politics in the whole situation. The Egyptians were tired of their colonial status and there had been some trouble in Cairo. Arthur tried to calm any fears Winifred might have:

If you see accounts of riots and strikes in Egypt don't worry about it. They're having a political crisis in Cairo just now, but there won't be any serious trouble, certainly not in this district, for everyone here is much too keen on attracting and fleecing the tourists!(57)

Questions of nationalistic feeling and *The Times* privileged position, provided difficult enough problems, but into this came a third and complex ingredient. This was 'the nagging question of the division of objects' or who would keep the treasures of the tomb of Tutankhamun. If the tomb was intact then under Egyptian Law the government could deny the claims of the excavators to a share of the excavated objects.(58) The tomb had been entered in antiquity, so was it intact or not? Ultimately, the contents of the tomb were to go to Cairo, although the whereabouts of certain objects, whose provenance is said to be from the tomb of Tutankhamun, which are not in Cairo, have continued to be controversial. This thorny subject is outwith the story of Mace, except to say that after Mace's death Winifred and Margaret visited Carter in London and Margaret still remembers her mother leaving in a very angry mood saying 'he should not have those things'.(59) In early 1923 it was not envisaged that the contents of the tomb would stay in Egypt in their entirety and Carter and Carnarvon began to squabble over the best way of dealing with the vexed question of the division. As Mace reported by 27 February not only was the *Morning Post* 'making all sorts of insinuations against the New York staff' but Carter and Carnarvon were 'barely speaking'.(60)

Squabbling and backbiting notwithstanding, the work had to continue and when Carter was away the burden fell on Mace. Until the decision to ban visitors from the tomb and the laboratory was made there was the problem of people wandering around the site. Many were VIPs from Europe, and the Egyptian government who had to be humoured and entertained, but it was often a tongue-biting exercise for those who were trying to do the work. Many, especially the wealthy Europeans, felt they had a right to be in on the action and they tried everyone's patience to the limit. There were trustees from the Metropolitan, like the Macys who were fortunately, said Mace, 'exceedingly nice' but there were others like the Museum's President Mr. De Forest, 'a most uninspiring person without any dignity to carry off his position' and 'I can't stand him at any price'.(61) These comments indicate how touchy everyone had become within the tense atmosphere of the excavation. On one occasion Arthur was able to tell Winifred that he worked under the gaze of 'an Earl, a Lady, a Sir and two Honourables', and he added, 'they were a beastly nuisance'.(62). The most persistent of all the visitors was the Queen of the Belgians; she was, said Mace 'embarrassingly keen on everything'. On 18 February the entire day was taken up with royalty; in the morning there was Queen Melika, the Sultana and widow of the late King, 'she's a pleasant little lady, talking fluent French'. The Queen of the Belgians visiting on the same day arrived in great state and was met by Carter and Carnarvon and toured the site. Mace found her extremely nice and natural. As he told Winifred that evening in a letter, 'ordinary titles were as common as dirt and it's surely archaeology de-luxe this, we shake hands with two Queens in the course of a day'.(63) After four or five regal visits Mace found his patience wearing very thin; 'the good lady' he reported 'is much too persistent'. On 9 March she paid a further visit to the laboratory to see a box unpacked, so they picked a very dull one, in which no harm could possibly be done, but 'to tell you the truth we are bored with her ... royalties haven't much consideration for other folk'. Perhaps it was this visit that prompted his 'tirade against visitors'.(64)

If royalty made a nuisance of themselves by appearing in person, mere mortals could take up the Egyptologists' time by letter. Among Arthur Mace's papers there exists an envelope labelled 'letters from cranks'. This contains letters, cards and telegrams to Carter and Carnarvon from all over the world. Some were from former Egyptian employees of Carter offering congratulations and requesting their positions back. Others were from retired people offering practical service like that from a veteran of the Russo-Japanese War who believed he would be of help as he 'knows the native and his ways'. Others were from school boys wanting help with essays and school projects and hoping for 'a small stone from the tomb'. Some had an eye for the commercial value of the discovery like that from California wanting to acquire exclusive rights for a motion picture about Tutankhamun. A request for 'exclusive style rights' provides an indication of the impact the discovery was to have on art and design of the period. Everything from cinema architecture, jewellery design and the new Duchess of York's trousseau were influenced by ancient Egypt. Imperial Laboratories of Kansas City, 'Quality is our standard', wrote to Carter with a proposition for a mail order souvenir business based on reproduction items from the tomb. In addition there were letters from people who were clearly disturbed, like Miss Lillian Pharaoh who claimed to be descended from Tutankhamun and included a photograph of herself in a classical pose to prove her point. From Paris there was note from 'Le premier Empereur Egyptien' with a message for his people explaining that he was the re-incarnation of 'Tut-Ank-Hamen'. There was Mrs. Webb who wrote to Carnarvon and Carter as her brothers and thanking them for not sending her any money 'as they would have it off me'. Rose Holloway wanted Mr. Carter to settle an argument 'as to whether it was

*Lillian Pharaoh. (From the collection of Margaret Orr)*

*A telegram found in Mace's papers in an envelope labelled 'Letters from Cranks'. (From the collection of Margaret Orr)*

| No. 53A | Orig'l No. 524 | Words 24 | Date Stamp | G.14 EGYPTIAN STATE TELEGRAPHS صالحة التلغرافات المصرية |
|---|---|---|---|---|

From. ld — To
At 11 25 — At
By D — By

REMARKS V E

17 FEB 923

To

Honorable Howard
Carter Luxor Egypt

Office of Origin New York — Date 17 — Time 3 45am

Offer ten thousand dollars and profit sharing
arrangements for exclusive motion picture
rights tutankhamens tomb cable reply.

Murray Jarsson

.S.R.—1346—20-21—10000 × 200

*Mace assists Carter to*
*pack Tutankhamun's bed.*
*(Courtesy of The Times)*

you or your brother Charley who boarded at Mrs. Bullards in 1888–1889'.
There were sad letters like that of Mrs. Piper, 'a woman in a very humble and
ordinary walk of life, no prospect of ever beholding glorious and mysterious
Egypt', who just wanted a little sand from the desert. Inevitably, there were
letters from those concerned with curses and the occult, particularly after
Carnarvon's death. A letter from Ireland believed Lord Carnarvon's death to
have been the result of failure to perform ceremonies 'calculated to placate any
Ka or Ka's that might be in the sepulchre'. A second letter from the same writer
in Dublin urged the importance of dealing with the Ka, but also 'the *really*
*important thing* is to get the assistance of one who can reach the *vital forces of*
*the earth* and who is able to communicate with the Ka'. An ordinary medium he
cautioned would be useless: it had to be someone who 'has power' who
'understands', preferably 'a native'. A telegram probably from the same source
added 'if trouble continues reseal tomb, pour milk, oil and wine at
threshold'.(65)

There was a more immediate threshold for the team to consider, that
which lay at the northern end of the ante-chamber into the burial chamber. The
threshold had been blocked with dry rough stones and plastered. As the team
gradually cleared the first chamber during January and early February 1923,
excitement mounted as to what lay beyond the sealed door. By 14 February
Arthur was able to tell Winifred that he had spent the morning waxing the last
bed and that the first chamber was practically empty apart from the two sentinel
statues of the King which guarded the entrance to the tomb proper. This would
be the high point of the seasons work, and this combined with all the underlying
problems fed an almost electric atmosphere in the Valley of the Kings. Arthur
wrote to Winifred:

> I hope tomorrow will go off all right for everybody's nerves are on edge and
> Carter is on the verge of a nervous breakdown I should say. He and Lord

Carnarvon are on edge with each other all the time. I shall be glad when it is over. It does seem funny to think that the whole world is on tip toe of excitement over what we are going to find when we take down the sealed door tomorrow ...(66)

Mace's field diary for 16 February recorded the opening; 'Helped Carter take down sealed door', and listed those present, 'Carnarvon, Lady Evelyn, Sir William Garstin, Breasted, Gardiner, Lacau, Lythgoe, Winlock, Burton, Lucas, Callender, Engelbach, Bethell, native Under Secretary of State and a few others'.(67) One might be forgiven for thinking Mace was a rather cold and unemotional man from this rather bleak diary entry. However, his letters home and a description written in Aswan conveyed his feelings more accurately and he confessed to Winifred that he 'was dead with excitement and fatigue' and that it was 'a day and no mistake'.(68)

The event took place in great secrecy so as to avoid the attentions of the newspaper men who had been camping around the tomb in expectation. By prior arrangement they met after an early lunch and by arriving at the tomb without warning failed to give the newspaper men time to make arrangements to send messages home. At 2.15 p.m. 'we all took our coats off and filed silently down into the tomb'. Carter had rigged up a stage to get at the upper part of the sealed door and put boarding up to protect the two statues of the King guarding the entrance. Chairs were provided for the visitors who sat behind a railing. Carter, Callender and Mace were the only ones working behind the railing. Carter made a short diplomatic speech aimed at the native minister and then Carnarvon 'alluded particularly to the part played by the Metropolitan Museum'. Then Carter stripped to his trousers and vest struck the first blow with a hammer and chisel, and eventually made the hole big enough to put a torch in and 'we could all see the huge wooden erection covered with gold leaf; evidently the tabernacle which covered the sarcophagus'. At this point Carter asked Mace to help him:

> ... and gradually we eased out and took away the huge stones the door was blocked with. It was hard work, for the stones were very heavy to lift, and we had to be very careful, lest one, or a piece of one, might fall and do damage.

Burton photographed the proceedings and Mace was caught looking anxious, although he later told Winifred that he heard Lacau say to someone 'Monsieur Mace est toujours calme'.

Some two hours later, they were 'dusty dishevelled and perspiring', but the hole was wide enough for Carter to squeeze into. One by one the assembled party went in and it was, said Mace 'Curious to watch them come out, without exception each person threw up his hands and gasped'. Mace and Lucas went in together. 'When my turn came I was simply taken off my feet. The things in the outer chamber, beautiful as they are gave no idea of what was inside'. There was just enough room to squeeze around the corner of the tabernacle and along the passage. The doors were open and within could be seen the second structure with sealed door and above it on a frame 'a pall dropping over it, of linen, spangled with gold stars'. Then confessed Mace he was 'knocked ... all of a heap', as he saw the shrine containing the canopic jars:

*Carter, assisted by Mace (right), removes the sealed door at the entrance to Tutankhamun's burial chamber, 1923. (Courtesy of The Illustrated London News Picture Library)*

I think it is the most beautiful thing I've ever seen anywhere. It was the shrine for the canopic jars. That itself was not so wonderful, but round it, free standing, one on each side, there were four statues of goddesses, most un-Egyptian in attitude and beautifully modelled.(69)

Round about the chamber there were objects and boxes, there were a number of chariots, a gold and ostrich feather fan and a number of boats. Mace felt his head reeling with excitement and he found a lump in his throat as he contemplated the sight he beheld and thought that with the exception of a hurried visit by thieves ten years after the King's death, no-one had set foot in the chamber since the King was laid to rest more that three thousand years before. It was after five o'clock when the party emerged from the tomb looking exhausted and dazed. That evening Carter dined at Metropolitan House and they all talked into the night 'more or less like crazy people'. Mace was convinced that anyone looking in would have thought them drunk. In a sense they were.

Clearing the burial chamber would have to wait until the next season. There was also the more sobering thought of the official opening with the ubiquitous Queen of the Belgians 'and goodness knows who else'. Of greater concern to Arthur was the knowledge that he was missing Margaret's birthday on 22 February. 'Don't I wish I was there' he wrote. He also had to give Winifred a pep talk about taking on too many activities like 'mothers unions and

*Looking through the door of the four gilded shrines to the sarcophagus, top to bottom, Callender, Carter and Mace.*

*Carter and Mace working above the sarcophagus.*

*(Courtesy of the Metropolitan Museum of Art, New York)*

THE UPPER EGYPT HOTELS Cº

**ASSOUAN**
CATARACT HOTEL
SAVOY HOTEL
GRAND HOTEL
**LUXOR**
LUXOR WINTER PALACE
LUXOR HOTEL
KARNAK HOTEL

IMP. P. ARNAUD, LYON PARIS

# CATARACT HOTEL

Assouan. March 3ʳᵈ

It seems a long while since the day of the opening, but it might be as well to get my impressions on paper, to keep as a record.

In the first place, we scored a great triumph over the newspaper men. They for some reason had got it into their heads that we were going to make a secret opening without any representative of the government being present, so for three or four days they hardly left the tomb. On the Friday they had no idea anything was up. We fixed it for the afternoon, so that the tourists would be out of the way. Sir William Garstin and two or three others came to join our lunch party, but they came straight, so were not seen arriving. After lunch we met by appointment Lacau, Engelbach, things' and that she was to stop worrying about money: 'we shall make out all right' he told her.(70) With all the excitement of the opening it was thought best to close the work down for a weeks holiday to allow everyone to calm down and regain their composure for a fresh start. By this time Carter was, according to Mace 'a nervous wreck'. Arthur decided he needed a few days break and would make a visit he had long promised himself to Aswan. Carnarvon and Lady Evelyn also decided upon Aswan and asked Mace to join them and even arranged his accommodation at the Cataract Hotel. Thus he told Winifred he would be holidaying 'in some style'. Originally Winlock was to go as well, which pleased Mace as he didn't 'fancy being tête-á-tête with Lord Carnarvon for a week'. He also thought Lady Evelyn to be rather 'empty headed' although he realised Carter was very fond of her. Winlock changed his mind at the last minute and Mace was stuck with the arrangements. In the event his time in Aswan with the Earl and his daughter was most enjoyable and refreshing. Together they visited the bazaars, went sailing and 'generally loafed about'. There was a trip to Elephantine Island and to Philae. Another member of the party was Sir Charles Cust, an equerry to the King, and so there was lots of royal gossip. In the calming atmosphere of Aswan, Carnarvon and Mace clearly hit it off:

> Carnarvon's a queer fish, but in spite of his oddities very lovable. He and Lady Evelyn are devoted to each other, she is somewhat spoilt and a bit slangy, but there's a lot of good stuff in her. They treat me like one of the family and say I must go to Highclere ...(71)

By 7 March, Mace was back in the laboratory working on the boxes and

*Mace recalls his impressions of the opening of the sealed door while staying with Lord Carnarvon at the Cataract Hotel, 1923. (From the collection of Margaret Orr)*

*The laboratory. (Courtesy of The Times)*

their contents. Carnarvon left Luxor for Cairo on 14 March and on 19 March Carter received a telegram from Lady Evelyn saying he was ill. Mace was concerned: 'I hope it's not serious for I like the man'.(72) Mace's concern for Carnarvon's health was genuine but he also feared the disruption to the work if Carter was delayed too long in Cairo. Carnarvon was of course dangerously ill. In all probability he was bitten by a mosquito while at Aswan. He subsequently cut into the bite with his razor and the wound became infected. Since a car accident Carnarvon had not enjoyed the best of health and in an era before antibiotics, infection was a serious problem. He soon developed complications. Mace's letters to Winifred chart the ups and downs of the Earl's last days. On 29 March, Carter wired Mace that there had been a turn for the worse and Mace told Winifred that it would be a miracle if he pulled through. Carnarvon died on 5 April. Mace wrote to his mother-in-law:

*Mace escorts a crated object from the tomb of Tutankhamun. (Courtesy of The Times)*

> We all felt Lord Carnarvon's death. I've seen a lot of him this winter of course and I had got quite fond of him. He was a queer person, but very lovable.(73)

In a letter the day after Carnarvon's death Winifred asked Arthur what the Earl's views 'on a future life' were. Arthur said he did not know but said that Lord

Carnarvon was one of the most superstitious men he had ever met. Perhaps he would have been intrigued by the knowledge that his own death was to become the focal point for all the subsequent curse stories.

With Carnarvon's illness, Carter was away for a month. Mace was left with the responsibility of continuing the work by himself, of dealing with visitors, coping with letters and working on the book. It was a major responsibility and, as he told his mother-in-law, gave him little opportunity for his own letters. The camp took on an end of season atmosphere as everyone began to look forward to summer at home. A 'washed out' looking Carter returned on 16 April and was delighted at Mace's progress in his absence. 'He was astonished to find out how much we had done and didn't expect to find us anywhere near so far along'.(74) The Egyptians were gradually paid off and the Americans and British began to leave for home. By the end of April Mace and Burton had the Metropolitan House all to themselves which they confessed to rather enjoy, Mace more so, once Harry's wife Minnie had departed. As an essentially solitary man, happy in his own company, Mace was at a loss to understand why the Winlocks, Hall, Hauser and Wilkinson were happy to sail on the same day on the same boat. 'You'd think', he told Winifred that, 'after a winter in the same house they would rather have travelled separately'. He and Carter made plans and wrote. In the evenings they played bridge with Lucas and Burton. This must have been relaxing given the complex shuffling of cards they had experienced that winter in the desert.

Howard Carter

H. E. Winlock    November 5th 1923

Helen Winlock,
Frances Winlock

Nina de Garis Davies

N. de Garis Davies

Mary Millman Harkness

Ed

Edw. S. Harkness

Lucy Tappan Lythgoe

Albert M. Lythgoe.

Arthur C. Mace.

Charlotte R. Stillman

Winifred M. Mace

A. Lucas.

M. E. Mace

A. R. Callender

Walter Hauser

C. K. Wilkinson

CHAPTER FIVE

# 'A beautiful
# wonderful party ...'

Tutankhamun
the second season, 1923–1924

Arthur Mace must have been particularly aware of the irony of fate throughout 1922–1923. On the one hand there was the excitement and limitless possibilities afforded by his work with Howard Carter and the tomb of Tutankhamun. Yet on the other hand the unpromising nature of his family life cannot have been far from his thoughts as he sat at his trestle workbench in the tomb of Seti II. The welfare of his younger daughter Anne was a constant worry. Care of a Downs Syndrome child is a difficult prospect to contemplate in the late twentieth century; it must have been even more problematic in the 1920s particularly when one worked abroad and relied heavily on the goodwill of parents-in-law for both practical and financial help. As Anne reached school age the problems intensified.

On top of this the year had seen both children with a succession of childish ailments culminating in Margaret's appendicitis. For convalescence she was sent to the coast. In September 1923 she was with Arthur's sister at Bacton in Norfolk, and 'contrived to pick up typhoid'. It was, Arthur confessed to Albert Lythgoe in a letter to the Metropolitan dated 18 October 1923, 'a time of great anxiety' and a particular blow as she had just 'got splendidly strong again'. Margaret was seriously ill with a constant temperature of over 105° for nearly a fortnight with a nurse in attendance night and day. Lythgoe was told that she 'had been pretty bad poor kid' - in fact she was close to death.(1) As she

*The first page of the Metropolitan House guest book. (Courtesy of the Metropolitan Museum of Art, New York, 1976, 200, gift of Charles Wilkinson)*

approaches her eightieth year Margaret still vividly recalls the gathering of family and clergy around her bed in prayer as they anticipated the end. Miraculously there was recovery, and by mid-October her temperature was down and the worst over. Arthur had to postpone his return to work on Tutankhamun and it looked as though Winifred would not be able to join him, but she desperately wanted to and asked the family doctors what they thought about Margaret going with her to Egypt. This might seem a strange destination for a typhoid convalescent but, in fact the doctors thought the dry heat of the desert would be ideal for her as would the psychological benefit of being with both her parents. By the late autumn of 1923, Margaret was well enough to travel. In December, mother and daughter left their house, at 14 Hill Road, St. John's Wood for a journey across Europe to the site of the world's most famous archaeological discovery.

In Calais the passport officials thought Margaret was a boy. Their confusion was understandable as Margaret was almost bald. One of the effects of typhoid is a patchy loss of hair. To prevent this and to ensure a more even growth her head had been shaved. Margaret must have been a curious sight. In Italy the train journey was broken for trips to the Alps and the Italian Lakes. At Trieste they were met by a horse and carriage and driven to an Italian boat. Despite being 'exorbitantly overcharged' by porters, Winifred was glad to be safely on board and delighted to find that Arthur (who was already in Egypt), had arranged two state rooms with beds and not bunks. 'I have never seen such luxury' Winifred wrote to her mother.(2) The sea was calm and the weather cool as the ship slipped its moorings. Unfortunately, as they sailed along the Dalmatian Coast the conditions became rough and a bemused and seasick Margaret was sent to bed supperless. By the time the ship had reached Brindisi Margaret had found her sea legs and was well enough to play on deck with her doll 'Molly'. Already Winifred believed the voyage was producing a noticeable improvement in her daughter's health. However, she was careful to keep her away from 'some terrible looking foreigners who travel fourth class and sleep on deck'.(3) To Winifred's relief there were some more suitable travelling companions on board including 'some fine old army and Diplomatic people and a nice girl who is going to study cotton for Professor Yod of Balliol'. The cotton student was a simple, clever and delightful girl who unlike the rest of Winifred's table companions 'refrained from airing all her knowledge'.(4)

On disembarking at Cairo's Port of Alexandria, they were met by an obviously excited Arthur. Winifred could hardly contain herself at the prospect of being back in noisy, dusty, exciting Cairo, 'a city which never sleeps and is even noisier now there are cars which have hooters far worse than ours'.(5) Accommodation had been arranged in The Continental Hotel and Winifred made sure she awoke early to open the shutters and look at the city, 'at its best, in a half light, over the gardens and minarets to the desert in the distance'.(6) The rather grand hotel impressed young Margaret who, with all the activity around her was able to forget the mosquito bites she soon acquired. In any case Winifred had remembered to pack iodine and citronella. At the Bazaar Winifred and Arthur were able to indulge in their love of Oriental carpets. Winifred was impressed with the Persian silk rugs which compared favourably with the pre-war prices. By her own admission she 'fell in love with a little one from Beluchistan'. To mark a successful bargaining session they were presented with sweet tea in glass cups and Turkish Delight for Margaret. Arthur thought it would be nice if his daughter learnt some Arabic and they began by leaving the carpet merchant with 'may your day be blessed'. The shopping expedition was followed by a visit to Cairo Museum so that Winifred could see the Tutankhamun objects from the first season's work. Despite her familiarity with Egyptian antiquities Winifred was clearly struck by the beauty of these objects. There were however, expressions of disappointment for the Museum's display techniques:

> I feel if only these beautiful things were shown as New York shows them (i.e.
> the Metropolitan), then we should see all the beauty, but as it is the lighting
> is poor and the frames of the cases so heavy.(7)

For Arthur, some of the time he spent with his family in Cairo involved business arrangements with Howard Carter. The relationship between Howard Carter and the Egyptian authorities was becoming ever more strained and the Museum officials and government authorities were making life increasingly difficult for the excavation team.

Carter had meetings with Lord Allenby the High Commissioner for Egypt in an attempt to ease the situation. Winifred believed the problems would not have been so great had Lord Carnarvon lived and certainly people like Pierre Lacau, Director General of the Antiquities Service 'would not have dared make such difficulties'.(8) This may or may not have been the case. As an English aristocrat Carnarvon may well have carried more weight and influence than Carter with all his enemies. It has to be said, however, that Carnarvon's handling of the vexed questions of press coverage, giving sole rights to *The Times* ensured a dignified and accurate coverage of the excavation but was hardly a diplomatic coup as far as the rest of Fleet Street, and indeed the Egyptians were concerned. In any case behind the personalities, the political tensions were such that clashes were inevitable. In 1922 there had been an acknowledgement of the independent status of the 'Veiled Protectorate' and the Egyptians were in the mood to flex their muscles.

Nevertheless Carter continued to exercise a 'where angels fear to tread' approach and Winifred was happy to report that Arthur at least acted as a restraining influence on him. Carter himself told Winifred 'that Arthur's advice behind him and fighting instincts had helped him through'.(9)

After a few days rest at The Continental Hotel, the Mace family left Cairo by train for Luxor. There was a dinner on board and then 'a sleeping car bigger than ordinary'. They awoke to 'watch the dawn slowly rising and the desert turning pink'. Winifred was pleased to see the Nile again and to find that the Winter Palace Hotel which she remembered as a rather stark new building before the war had mellowed with age assisted by the bougainvillae cascading over the staircases. Other guests at the hotel included; Professor Percy Newberry (1869–1949) the Botanist and Egyptologist and his wife Essie (a skilled embroideress who was to work on the pall covering the burial shrine), Professor Alan Gardiner (1879–1963) the expert on Egyptian inscriptions and language, Mrs. Merton wife of *The Times* correspondent and Mrs. Scott wife of a British Museum scientist who was unwell with a chill and carbuncle. This state of affairs noted the stoic Winifred was 'hardly a good start'.(10)

The following day they made their way across the river which Winifred 'always loved'. She was then amused to find they had to be carried ashore and that 'this made the maids squeal'. With the Harknesses and their chauffeur Ellis they drove to the Metropolitan House, a building which impressed Winifred and which she described to her mother:

> ... most charming with furniture suitable for it and lovely cushions of Bochara work, beautiful hanging lamps, old woodwork in the hall and dining room; the fireplace has a set of de Morgan tiles over it. Mr. Winlock certainly did it most artistically.(11)

Their rooms opened out on to a verandah looking to the high desert on one side and, to the other the magnificent temple complex of Deir-el-Bahri. This area was traditionally connected with the cult of the cow goddess Hathor and was the site of the mortuary temples of Nebhepetrec Mentuhotpe of the XI Dynasty and Queen Hatshepsut of the XVIII Dynasty. Not only was there a room with a view but the view was from a bright airy playroom, ideal for Margaret. Fortunately too, Margaret was to have a playmate as Frances, the daughter of Herbert and Helen Winlock, was also there for the winter.

Metropolitan House was a busy place in December 1923. Among the others who made it their temporary home that winter were Albert and Lucy Lythgoe, Minnie and Harry Burton, Walter Hauser and Edward and Mary Harkness. Winifred and Arthur seemed to have a particular affinity with the Harknesses. Winifred wrote to her mother that of all the Americans and millionaires she had ever met they were the nicest! Harkness was in fact a millionaire many times over. He had inherited his fortune from his father Stephen who was the wealthiest of John D. Rockefeller's Standard Oil partners. During his life time it was estimated that he gave away in philanthropic bequests

*Interior of the Metropolitan House. (Courtesy of the Egyptian Expedition, Metropolitan Museum of Art, New York)*

*Staff of the Metropolitan House. (From the collection of Margaret Orr)*

over $100,000,000. In most cases Harkness played little or no part in the organisations that benefited from his philanthropy. His trusteeship of the Metropolitan Museum and his interest in the Egyptian Department seems to have been an exception to this general rule. The latter being largely the result of his and his wife's very close friendship with Albert and Lucy Lythgoe.(12) Not surprisingly the Harknesses and Mrs. Harkness's sister Charlotte travelled in style. They had their own Nile boat 'Chonsu' as well as their car and chauffeur Ellis. Ellis was a firm favourite with the children; as well as driving them to Luxor for shopping trips, he helped them to ride camels and even trimmed Margaret's hair as it began to grow.

With Christmas only days away there were enthusiastic preparations at Metropolitan House. There was also a slight feeling of despondency among the team as work increasingly took second place to the problems with the authorities. Winifred wrote on 23 December, 'work has been so delayed and there are so many troubles, Mr. Carter might even close the work down'.(13) Winifred was saddened by this prospect because of the amount of effort and co-operation that had gone into the whole undertaking, 'the work has never been done so wonderfully, the best expert for each section, Professor Gardiner for inscriptions, Professor Newberry for botany, all waiting the other side for the work'.(14)

Perhaps because the work was proceeding at a slower pace, Howard Carter took Winifred and Margaret down to the Valley of the Kings in his car to see the Tomb of Tutankhamun. Margaret remembered the valley being 'deep and frightening' and that the journey lasted about twenty minutes. Winifred was disappointed to find the tomb spoiled by scaffolding, but 'the blaze of gold and glorious blue faience is startling!'. Carter showed them one of the shrines and opened the doors wide enough to see the 'beautiful untarnished gold doors of the inner shrine'.(15) At the burial shrine Winifred climbed three steps and:

> ... with a torch looked between the cover and the shrine which is bolstered up by beams and there lay the palls of linen, dark brown with age studded with gold buttons as were on the wig of little Senebtisi fifteen years ago, in front of the great doors the pall fell to pieces but the ingenious man has a plan to save the rest ...

Winifred was particularly impressed when Carter showed her two simple alabaster vases one of which was a lotus flower, 'two buds and open leaves below'.(16) They then walked up to the tomb laboratory:

> So that I could see my father treating the chariots, they were gorgeous, gold, with pictures of people, Negroes, Asiatics, prisoners, and outside ornamentation of lotus flowers, daisies, lotus leaves in faience glass and carnelian. The wheels were covered in sheet gold.(17)

*Margaret, with her hair beginning to grow, poses with Frances Winlock and Ellis the chauffeur outside the Metropolitan House. (From the collection of Margaret Orr)*

Winifred commented on how well set out the laboratory was, 'all beautifully planned, rooms, shelves, nests of boxes, carpenters busy close by, everything just so'. With pride Winifred was able to tell her mother, 'Here Arthur reigns supreme, the chariots are gorgeous ... I have never seen such things'.(18) As they watched Arthur and Lucas, assisted by Richard Bethell, working quickly with simple conservation techniques, most impressed, Winifred noted, 'hot wax was poured on from a bronchitis kettle shaped receptacle'.(19)

Christmas 1923 was certainly a much happier celebration for Arthur and his family than that of the previous year. There was a party on Christmas Eve in the Winter Palace Hotel, complete with Christmas tree, carol singing and a Bishop. Margaret and Frances woke early on Christmas Day to find stockings hanging in the dinning room in the American fashion. They were filled with little things Winifred had carefully secreted in her trunks as she packed in St. John's Wood. The girls were particularly delighted with the presents they received from Mrs. Harkness, gold bangles with seed pearls and unpolished turquoise. Christmas lunch was a family picnic at the Ramesseum, 'a wonderful pile of ruins built by Ramesses the Great'. When the Mace family returned to the house they found Lucy Lythgoe making table decorations and with Ellis they helped to decorate the Dome Room with red streamers. 'Never', wrote Winifred, 'had a camp, if one could call this a camp, kept Christmas with such vigour'. That night there were eighteen at Metropolitan House for a dinner, after which there were party games. Howard Carter threw himself enthusiastically into 'playing the most childish games', including dumb crambo.(20)

Once Christmas and New Year were over, the team settled down to work and for the children there were lessons and exciting new experiences. As Margaret played dolls with her new found friend the whole thing seemed at times to be one long 'beautiful wonderful party'. Nevertheless the Maces and the Winlocks tried hard to see that the children were not spoilt and that their day

*Carter supervises the packing of objects while Margaret is distracted by other activities. (From the collection of Margaret Orr)*

Dec 23rd

El assassif
Luscor
Upper Egypt

Dearest Mother
The mail days come very close which is a pity
so you may have long gaps to wait.
Try as we will we cannot believe Xmas is so near, I have
just put the stockings together & they are to hang American
fashion over the dining room chimney mantle piece
The children have been very busy putting up parcels & the
other afternoon's shopping with Ellis was a great success
(he is the Harkness's chauffeur) Frances bargained for necklaces
which caused great amusement to her Father, having Marg:
made her bold also they were taken for Ellis's little girls in
the boat. We were 13 to lunch yesterday including Prof:
Newberry, Mr Merton & an Inspector each tea various people
turned up; some yesterday from Liverpool, one who knew
Mr Allen who I met at Cranhand. It is amusing looking
at the various get-ups people come in mostly like
Mr Harkness's sister in plain tailor made & exactly hat-
others in woollen jumpers & knicker bockers for riding others
in pretty summer frocks with too much jewellery, one
with a diamond butterfly on her shoulder which was
unwise among natives, I shall be very sorry when Mrs
Lythgoe goes she is a good hostess & treats her guests
with great decense, Miss Still man Mr Harkness's sister
is very nice, not so highly nervous as Mrs H, she has been

---

*A page from one of Winifred's letters to her mother (Mrs. Blyth) describing the fashions of the ladies and the preparations for Christmas, 1923. (From the collection of Margaret Orr)*

had some structure to it and above all that their education continued. They were kept away from the adults as much as possible and took their simple meals separately. Each day, two hours were spent on lessons. For some subjects the setting was ideal:

> ... I have a delightful American book on the history of mankind which Margaret can easily understand and loves it, so History, Religion and Geography is being worked together on the site of the first civilisation.(21)

Winifred concentrated on History and English and spent a great deal of her time reading to the children. A particular favourite of both her and the children was F. H. Burnett's *Secret Garden*. Meanwhile Helen Winlock saw to the artistic content of the curriculum and supervised painting and drawing lessons, which were usually in the form of field trips.

Away from the lessons there were outings. Winifred always enjoyed crossing the Nile to Luxor: 'I love that river' she wrote to her mother. 'It is an exquisite scene - how often Americans use that word exquisite and it is so lovely nothing else quite describes it'.(22) In Luxor there was shopping and then

*Outside the Metropolitan House, Margaret and Frances with their dolls are pictured with Helen Winlock and Winifred and Arthur Mace.*

*The only way to travel – Margaret and Frances with Ellis the chauffeur.*

*(From the collection of Margaret Orr)*

a visit to the hairdresser at the Winter Palace before lunch in the Grill Room and finally afternoon tea before the trip home. These excursions were not without their dangers particularly when they drove past the sugar cane plantations which provided ideal cover for bandits preying on wealthy travellers. For this reason it was necessary to take an armed guard. There were lots of picnics and sketching outings. Margaret liked to go to Medinet Habu, the mortuary temple of King Ramesses III. Here they found a little courtyard with broken columns which they could use as tables and:

> ... We drew and painted and were read to. Frances having been before had
> set out with sketching book, writing pad, skipping rope, sunshade, fly switch
> and dark glasses. We had sandwiches and then tinned pears. Later we found
> another court looking into what all those years ago was an ornamental pool
> on which they'd have flamingos, barges and beyond a walled garden.(23)

A letter of Winifred's also mentions this outing and her suggestion that the girls play Kings and Queens:

> ... so we went round to the Palace side where are the bases of three thrones
> and also two baths ... the guard came round and was amused at the game, but
> he warned the children of scorpions among the stones.(24)

There were also the mundane tasks to attend to like sewing and pressing as well as the regular letters home to Granny Blyth in Walsall. From time to time there were problems arising from the care and education of Anne which required attention. For relaxation Winifred rode Howard Carter's donkey and in the evening the adults played cards or mah-jong. Domestic life, however, was constantly disrupted by the arrival of visitors and Winifred was expected to play a part in their entertainment under the guiding hand of Lucy Lythgoe. During the winter of 1923–24 Winifred noted the arrivals and departures of a number of illustrious visitors such as Prince Arthur (Duke of Connaught a son of Queen Victoria), the Astor family, the Monds, Sir Rider Haggard (who was, said Winifred, not a very interesting old man), and a cousin of the Kaiser. Egypt had long been on the itinerary of well-heeled Europeans and an invitation to visit the tomb of Tutankhamun was highly sought after. The visitors were not always a success with those living in Metropolitan House - they got in the way, could be overbearing, or just plain boring like Rider Haggard. Occasionally, the guests were unintentionally amusing such as Lord Astor, 'a tall man, very quiet - with a false leg and he can do everything'. Winifred believed he had 'three different legs for different occasions'.(25) A visit from Sir Herbert and Lady Samuel was less appreciated; 'Arthur said his son called him the Commissioner, which was certainly snobbish'. Winifred it has to be said was not entirely free from being snobbish or indeed from displaying what one might call period attitudes. The Samuels were described as '... very plain Jews, homely, I think you might say'. Winifred knew enough Americans and had enough experience of America to know that 'homely' has a much more critical connotation in the United States than it does in Britain. Such attitudes were common place among the English upper-middle classes of the period. Winifred was even more scathing about Robert Mond and his party:

*Winifred (standing right) helps to entertain H. Rider Haggard (seated) with other members of the expedition, including Minnie Burton (seated left). (Courtesy of the Egyptian Expedition, Metropolitan Museum of Art, New York)*

... he is doing a small excavation at the back of the Ramesseum, he is the brother of Alfred Mond, the ladies wear pearls as big as eggs on their fingers!(26)

In fact, Mond's contribution to Egyptology in practical and financial terms was considerable. In his work on the Theban Tombs he had been assisted by among others both Carter and Newberry. He made generous donations to many museums and became president of the Egypt Exploration Society in 1929.(27)

Winifred's attitude towards the Egyptians might also be described as one which was firmly rooted in its time and one which she doubtless shared with others on the excavation. It was the product of years of British supremacy and imperialism. Winifred was pleased that her daughter was 'not at all alarmed by dusky faces', but at the same time made sure Margaret was kept well away from native children. Her lack of faith in the Egyptians as possible masters of their own fate was given voice in a letter to Walsall which commented on the elections, '... if you knew how they were conducted you could see the country will stand a poor chance in the hands of its own people'. To make matters worse

*Frances, Margaret and Winifred with Mrs. Merton (wife of The Times correspondent) at Luxor. (Courtesy of the Egyptian Expedition, Metropolitan Museum of Art, New York)*

she noted the growing tendency to cultivate opium.(28) Natives were inevitably dirty and Egyptian children dressed in awful frocks and loud colours. It would be unwise to read too much into this, Winifred's prejudices were those of her class and her time. Indeed her attitude to Egypt and the Egyptians was probably more positive and well disposed than that of many of her contemporaries. Winifred's carping comments can equally be matched by those which show her enthusiasm for her husband's workplace and its people. Her strong attachment to the river has already been noted and she also commented about how stately and graceful she found the Egyptians. Inevitably the political problems surrounding the excavations exacerbated feelings and prejudices. When Lythgoe, Carter and Mace went to Luxor to see the Minister's secretary they were incensed by his attitude and the fact that he appeared to laugh at them. This led an indignant Winifred to describe him as 'a fat blackamoor'. In spite of this Winifred continued to encourage Margaret to learn Arabic and was delighted when she discovered that the Egyptians called her 'Meragmese', the wife of Mace.(29)

Socially, the event of the season was a fantasia or native entertainment. On 22 January 1924, it was timed to coincide with Edward Harkness's birthday. Winifred seemed to have particularly appreciated the colour and spectacle of this event which included jugglers as well as singers and dancers:

> The band consists of a drum and three pipers, they breathe through their noses and the cheeks are distended like apples, they go on without a break. I suppose most people would say what a noise, but after a while there is a fascination in the repetition ... the chief singer and his reed player were always to be remembered: I heard Arthur say to Mrs. Davies much the same scene was acted four thousand years ago, the blind harper and the reed player, the singing and the dancing, she is copying these scenes so often in her copies of the tombs around here.(30)

*Watching the 'fantasia' organised for Mr. Harkness on his birthday are Arthur Mace, Frances Winlock and Margaret Mace. (From the collection of Margaret Orr)*

That evening there was a dinner with an Arabian flavour: lentil soup, a Nile fish and a whole lamb roasted with stuffed tomatoes and cucumbers. Margaret and Frances helped with the organisation by cutting out place card settings:

> Margaret did me a donkey beautifully, Arthur did not believe she drew it. Frances planned a camera one for Mr. Burton, beads for Arthur, medicine roll for Mr. Hauser, and a foundation deposit for Mr. Winlock.(31)

*Left: Ready to embark on Harkness's Nile boat 'Chonsu'. (From the collection of Margaret Orr)*

*On board 'Chonsu', Arthur and Winifred seated in the distance. (Courtesy of the Egyptian Expedition, Metropolitan Museum of Art, New York)*

Harkness was much moved. He proposed a toast to the children and then invited the whole party to spend a day on his boat. Winifred was able to end a letter of 23 January by telling her mother that 'the children felt there was still more to live for'. Margaret Mace vividly recalled the trip and remembered the elegantly-dressed adults and eating the tiniest of sandwiches as 'Chonsu' drifted along the Nile.(32)

Another party which was remembered by Margaret was that which she and Frances gave Howard Carter. Following their visit to the tomb of Tutankhamun, Margaret and Frances set up their own excavation. They enthusiastically organised wooden trays of cotton wool and bandages just as they had witnessed in the tomb and the laboratory. The adults were willing to indulge the children and helped them to tidy up the play room and set tea for four. Mr. Merton, *The Times* correspondent, arrived to write an article about their tomb work and Howard Carter acted as Inspector of Antiquities. With them were Arthur, Mr. Lucas and Mr. Bethell. What a strange little party it must have been, a pretty dark-haired American schoolgirl, her tomboyish looking new friend from England, their dolls and the man who found the tomb of Tutankhamun.(33)

*Right: Paying a visit to Mr. Winlock's dig are Winifred Mace (with sun shade), Lucy Lythgoe (with fly switch) and Mary Harkness. (From the collection of Margaret Orr)*

Life in and around the Metropolitan House and in the Valley of the Kings was not always blessed with a party atmosphere. This was hardly surprising, because living and working away from home for long periods is not easy even for seasoned field archaeologists. For the Europeans, life in Egypt required a degree of dedication, the physical climate could be difficult, and in the early 1920s the political climate was such that the excavation was not particularly welcomed by the authorities. Inevitably, there were tensions among the Europeans themselves, particularly as a number of strong personalities were living under the same roof. Like colonials everywhere, they attempted to keep up a western lifestyle, observing the rituals of polite society at home with afternoon tea and dressing for dinner. There must have been many occasions when the veneer slipped. There was always the slight degree of awkwardness with the Winlocks. Clearly Winifred respected Herbert Winlock, she admired both his 'quickness of brain' and his digging 'so beautifully done' but she found him 'grouchy' and believed he was jealous of Arthur's involvement in Tutankhamun.(34) Evidence of Herbert's difficult temperament is found in the fact that Frances frequently joined Winifred, Arthur and Margaret for breakfast as he was always particularly awkward in the morning.(35) Winifred and Helen Winlock spent a great deal of their time together and seemed to have developed quite a good relationship. Winifred believed, however, that Helen lacked a sense of responsibility when it came to acting as head of the house during Mrs. Lythgoe's absence. Margaret Mace remembered her as a pretty artistic lady with sparkling blue eyes, a love of children, of riding and of painting, but, 'she was no housewife'.(36) It has to be said that Winifred had a tendency to be over critical (this became more noticeable after her husband's death) and she believed Helen Winlock to be quite the untidiest person in the camp. In her favour, however, was her kindness to Margaret and above all her breeding which was 'quite the best in the camp'.(37)

When problems did arise they were often smoothed out by Lucy Lythgoe. Lucy was very much the 'Queen Bee' when it came to day to day affairs of life in the House. Winifred approved of this state of affairs. The relationship between Mace and Lythgoe had always been good. Winifred believed Lucy to be 'a good manager and a great leavener'. An efficient manager was probably a good thing given some of the temperaments in the House and also because there were those like Mrs. Harkness and her sister Charlotte Stillman who were rather nervous and therefore unsettling characters. Lucy's position in the camp hierarchy was said to be coveted by Minnie Burton, wife of the photographer Harry. The 'slender, quite handsome, and well-dressed' Harry was liked and respected by everyone.(38) Minnie the equally well dressed and upright daughter of a British army officer seems to have inspired little affection. Margaret Mace remembered her as terribly social and rather domineering. Winifred's letters speak of her fearful temper; 'Mrs. Burton I really don't talk to, she is like a volcano ...'. On another occasion dreading the departure of Lucy Lythgoe she wrote 'Mrs. Burton is a horror, I just keep out of her way'.(39)

Surprisingly, perhaps, Winifred did not keep out of Howard Carter's way.  Indeed she seems to have had a degree of empathy with, as well as a high opinion of, this enigmatic character. They talked a great deal about birds together and his artistic interests and talents will have appealed to her. Neither

*The Metropolitan team (1924–1925), the year after the Maces left, with Frances Winlock and her sister. (Courtesy of the Egyptian Expedition, Metropolitan Museum of Art, New York)*

was fond of 'living in a crowd'. Carter allowed Winifred to ride his donkey which she did two or three times a week and he always showed an interest in the children. This he demonstrated by his guided tour of the tomb, his visit to the children's tea party and his involvement in the social activities of Metropolitan House. There was a considerable degree of admiration for his ingenuity and his willingness to 'tackle problems where other people would have employed engineers'. Winifred observed that he frequently undertook hard manual labour himself, indeed 'lifting weights he should not lift'. At the same time he was able to handle the most delicate of objects. Winifred soon realised that while he had to suffer many indignities heaped upon him by the Egyptian authorities, he was his own worst enemy. He was both sensitive and intolerant. He was an autocrat and when 'he was thwarted at every turn ... all reason was taken from him'. Carter, she soon realised, had spent thirty years in Egypt antagonising people and had built up much resentment. He had, she wrote '... always gone his own way, so clever he could do anything ... and found it hard not to quarrel with everyone'. He was possibly the worst person to have to deal with the Egyptian authorities.(40)

Personalities and politics notwithstanding, work on the tomb continued at times slowly and with numerous interruptions. Accounts of Arthur's works in his own words are lacking for this period. Winifred saw to the duty letters home and there was no need to write to Lythgoe as he was also in Thebes. The first volume of Carter and Mace's *The Tomb of Tutankhamun* was selling well and Winifred was able to tell her mother that Arthur was listed among the bestsellers in Paris.(41) As well as working on the chariots, Arthur began to treat the magnificent life-sized statues of the King which were of black wood and gilded plaster. The ladies made periodic trips to the tomb and on 31 January watched the unwrapping of ceremonial sticks discovered between the first and second shrines:

> The cloth the sticks were in was all falling away, but one bundle was sealed, two sticks were alone, and when the black from the cloth was brushed off, they were perfect, one long gold stick, one silver with a perfect figure of the king ... (42)

While the sticks were being unwrapped Winifred sat next to *The Times* correspondent, Mr. Merton, who told her he had not enough adjectives to describe the pieces. Winifred told her mother that it was Arthur's belief that he used too many adjectives already in his descriptions and agreed that she had grown tired of reading 'spellbound' herself.(43) The wives also paid visits to Mr. Winlock's excavation particularly when important finds were made. On 10 February they went to see, 'rows of stumps of trees and two ponds used for lilies certainly Hatshepsut's temple must have been lovely'.(44)

The highlight of the season's work was to have been the raising of the sarcophagus lid, but as the political situation approached a climax, the event was not all it might have been. For Carter the final insult came with a directive from Cairo saying who was to be present at the event and in particular that the wives of the archaeologists were not to be there. Carter was so enraged by this that 'looking desperately ill and in a fury' he threatened to shut the tomb down and indicated that Mace and Burton would resign. Carter, Lythgoe and Mace went to

Cairo to see the Minister and on 12 February, the lid was raised without the wives being present:

> ... Arthur and Mr. Carter rolled cloth back and the coffin lay intact, wood and
> gold leaf and gold modelled likenesses - a wreath of flowers I think round the
> Cobra on his forehead. Then all was lowered again.(45)

It must have been such a sad occasion, '... as Arthur says the dream of every Egyptologist has been spoilt by jealousy'.(46)

As if to antagonise Carter even further, on the evening of the opening he received a note forbidding the ladies to go to the tomb at all. Carter 'in speechless fury' went to Luxor and told the Minister's secretary that this last insult could not be overlooked and that he was keeping the keys of the tomb and that his collaborators had resigned. Professor Gardiner decided to ask Pierre Lacau the Director of Antiquities quite pointedly if they were trying to oust Carter. Lacau admitted that if Carter did not agree to many new regulations the Ministry would take the tomb over and Carter would be asked to work for them. 'This', Winifred wrote was because 'they had no experts to deal with it'. She could not help but be amused by this convoluted thinking which she regarded as typically oriental. In the end of course the Ministry did not take over the administration of the excavation. Lythgoe believed this was primarily due to Mace:

> As near as I can size the situation up, ... when they went up to Luxor to make
> that inventory of the tomb, (they) were so impressed by your records and
> methods of work all through, that none of them wants to be called upon to
> take a hand. Comparisons might prove to their disadvantage in other
> words.(47)

Rubbing salt into Carter's wounds, the authorities did not wait to see if he dared to disobey them, but sent ten soldiers and three inspectors to guard the tomb and Winifred admitted to feeling very depressed about the whole situation:

> I fear it may end very badly and Carter will be forced to give the whole thing
> up. Arthur has left his work all about ... ready to mend, his beautiful gold and
> silver sticks left covered up, his notes all left;  there will be no more work
> done this season and maybe not anymore. Mr. Carter said sadly to Arthur
> today 'I am a nuisance to myself and to my friends'. The sarcophagus lid is
> suspended in mid-air by three pulleys, what if it breaks! I must stop I feel too
> sad that such a momentous piece of work maybe lost; of course if Arthur and
> Mr. Burton offered to work for the government they would snatch at it.
> Goodnight.(48)

Carter shut himself away in his house and would only see Arthur. The rest of the camp endeavoured to make the best of things. Winifred went to Luxor for the day and detected an anti-British atmosphere which she felt was directly related to the fuss over the tomb. The children still had to be entertained, so they took their sketch pads to Medinet Habu and sat in Ramesses III's Harim boiling eggs. Meanwhile Arthur tried to help Carter prepare statements for the lawyers and found himself despairing as he attempted to steer Carter on a diplomatic course. He also tried to encourage him to paint. An unfinished watercolour by Carter was rescued from the waste paper basket by Mace. As frustrations mounted so the desert climate seemed to mirror the difficulties of the European visitors:

> This stewing heat has come so suddenly and we have had no let up for a week. It is impossible outside for flies and even at night with the door open there is little air, the children are quite well, but look washed out, last night we stood on the hill at the back of the house looking over the wonderful landscape feeling very sad. The country Arthur has loved he begins to hate ...(49)

Arthur, Winifred and Margaret were with Carter at his house on the evening that the Government demanded the keys and entered the tomb. They stood and watched in the dark as the lights of the car full of Ministers and Pierre Lacau approached, followed by a carriage full of soldiers and a camel corps. The Egyptian Government was soon to realise the enormity of the task and that Carter and his American colleagues were essential. At the time, however, the situation looked bleak. The strain began to tell on both Carter and Mace. Carter developed pleurisy and Arthur's never robust constitution began to weaken under the strain. Odd days were spent in bed and he became increasingly thin.

With or without problems the digging season was drawing to a close and the thoughts of the guests at Metropolitan House began to turn to home. Before this, however, there was another diversion in the form of Margaret Mace's eleventh birthday. Winifred managed to arrange a small party with the children of an inspector and a mission doctor in Luxor. Everyone enjoyed themselves and behaved well, 'even Mrs. Burton'. Minnie gave Margaret a bangle of gold wire and elephant hair and Helen Winlock made a doll's sofa, chair and bed.(50)

Arthur Mace and his family left Egypt at the beginning of March. They decided to go home via Italy in the hope that a short holiday would benefit Arthur. Winifred felt really sad to be leaving her 'wonderful valley', and the children who had become firm friends, hated parting. Arthur had gone on ahead to Cairo to make arrangements and when they met up Winifred was alarmed to find Arthur looking so thin and unwell. On their Italian boat 'Scilia' she found herself nursing not only her seasick daughter but her exhausted husband too. In addition Winifred found Americans on the boat 'who can be so tiring when you have invalids' and worse still, thirty Germans, 'you can imagine the feeling of the few English', she wrote to her mother, 'the same fat, bejewelled bad-mannered people'. To add to the general levity of the situation Winifred discovered that an old man died of pneumonia on board. The weather was rough and bitterly cold and when they arrived in Naples it was lashing with rain.(51)

Fortunately, the accommodation helped to cheer everyone up. They stayed firstly at the Grand Hotel in Genoa, which was 'really Italian, delicious wholesome cooking, hot and cold running water and lots of cats'. By 14 March, they were in the Hotel Parragi in Santa Margherita Ligure, near Genoa, an area Arthur knew well from his war service. It was said Winifred liked a stage setting and she clearly adored her little hotel with its little red tiles and green shutters. Sustained by Valentine's Meat Extract, Arthur was able to sleep in the sun surrounded by olives, peach blossom, campanula and violets. From time to time there was news from Cairo. They were appalled by news of 'a scandalous letter from Arthur Weigall' who had been the *Daily Mail's* correspondent '... he did more mischief than any man ... words fail everyone who knows the man'. On the other hand Margaret received a postcard from Frances saying 'I think they will give Mr. Carter the tomb back'.(52)

As a period of convalescence the holiday in Italy appears to have been something of a disaster. The weather continued to be appalling. There was a cyclone in Amalfi and Winifred believed it was the worst winter in Italy since 1917. Arthur's health was erratic and several attempts to leave for England had to be aborted because he was so ill. Winifred wrote; 'I think anxiety tells on him badly and the worry of the tomb on top of Margaret's illness was too much'. On 14 April, Arthur wrote to his mother-in-law, 'The fates seem against us don't they?'(53)

*An informal snapshot of Margaret almost back to full health. (From the collection of Margaret Orr)*

CHAPTER SIX

# After
# Tutankhamun

If Arthur and Winifred were at all superstitious then they might have been forgiven for believing that the storms of the Italian spring were portents of things to come. The next four years were to be difficult and depressing for them both. Winifred wrote to her mother from Italy:

> I hope this will do him good, he easily gets tired so he wants to stay until he gets better - I daresay a month in bed would do him good. After this winter he feels he can never go back to Egypt, so I don't know what will happen.(1)

Mace's premonitions about not returning to Egypt were correct. His health suffered a complete breakdown. The next few years were spent in England, on the Riviera, in Switzerland and in New York. It was a measure of the high esteem in which he was held that his continuing salary and these trips were paid for by the Trustees of the Metropolitan Museum of Art or by Edward Harkness. Harkness was particularly keen that he should be afforded every opportunity to return to full health. It was even suggested that California might provide the ideal climate in which he could write. Harkness made sure he had a chauffeur driven car and probably helped him to buy Sharrow, a large and rather pretty house near Haywards Heath in Sussex. Photographs of these years show him sitting in the garden looking pale and drawn while Margaret and Anne played round him. If there was to be any compensation for these years of ill-health then surely it was that of having the whole family close at hand.

*A pale and drawn Arthur sitting in the garden at Sharrow. (From the collection of Margaret Orr)*

*A miniature painting of Margaret on her return from Egypt. (From the collection of Margaret Orr)*

*Right: Winifred, Arthur and Anne in their Sussex garden.*

*A failing Arthur with his daughters at home in Sussex.*

*(From the collection of Margaret Orr)*

During this period, he made several attempts to prepare his notes on the Lisht pyramid for publication. He was frustrated to find he just did not have the strength for the task. Colleagues tried to encourage him. Harkness paid visits to Sharrow and Lythgoe corresponded regularly. Even Howard Carter made the effort to visit Sharrow, as Mace told Lythgoe:

> Carter came down a few days after he got back looking extremely fit and well. How does he do it? He has extraordinary recuperative powers, and I realise now how unnecessary it is for anyone to try and shoulder his worries for him.(2)

The same restorative powers were not possessed by Mace and his correspondence to his friend Lythgoe became more and more preoccupied with details of his health. On 14 January 1927, he wrote from Sharrow that he was 'still breathless and suffering from indigestion'; it was he believed 'a heritage of the arsenic poisoning' and he talked of seeing a heart specialist.(3) It is not clear

how he got arsenic poisoning. In the days before antibiotics it was sometimes used in small doses as a medicine, and it was used in museums, but principally by taxidermists. The effects of arsenic poisoning are very unpleasant and can prove fatal.(4) The heart specialist diagnosed thickening of the arteries 'due partly he thought to my long time in Egypt'.(5) Later that year he described his condition to Lythgoe as 'similar to that suffered by miners and caused by swallowing too much sand and dust in Egypt'.(6) There seemed to be a desperate need to detail the state of his health, in all probability as much to justify the position to himself as to give Lythgoe information:

> That last winter I had at Lisht I spent weeks underground making my lungs black by blowing decayed coffin dust into them and on the tomb work I spent most of my time breathing cloth dust.(7)

Given Lythgoe's thoughtfulness, he must have felt concerned about his friend.

By the autumn of 1927 Mace was in Kent Lodge a nursing home in Westgate-on-Sea. Watching him as he became thinner and weaker were Winifred and the girls. Margaret visited her father in October and Winifred told Edward Harkness what 'a terrible blow' it was for her to see him so helpless.(8) In early December Winifred's letters were written full of despair, '... the whole thing is a nightmare with little hope for the future'. To make matters worse, and unknown to Arthur, Winifred was herself seriously ill. Although the exact nature of her illness was not disclosed, clearly by the spring of 1928 she required surgery. Unable to go to London to see a doctor without Arthur knowing, she went home to Walsall on the pretext of visiting her mother. In Birmingham she

*Arthur with Winifred outside the nursing home at Westgate on Sea, shortly before his death. (From the collection of Margaret Orr)*

saw a specialist who decided to operate. Winifred arranged to have the surgery in Arthur's nursing home, 'with one of our very best men on stomach cases Sir Lenthal Chartle', and she was booked into the neighbouring room as Mrs. Johnson. Arthur was later able to tell the Lythgoes that the surgeon found 'two cysts which they removed, also other things and just to show there was no ill-feeling they took her appendix too'. When Arthur found out that his neighbour, Mrs. Johnson, was in fact his wife, he wrote to Lythgoe full of admiration for her courage and her concern that he should be kept free from worry. He was amused to find later that the letters he had written and stamped for Walsall were in fact promptly delivered to the next room. In a letter of 14 March 1928, to Lucy Lythgoe, Arthur gave Winifred rave reviews for her performance.(9) There was, after more than twenty years of marriage a great deal of love, affection and mutual admiration between the two. Arthur's letter to Lucy was to be his last to his friends in New York. The next message from England in Mace's file in the Metropolitan, was a telegram from Winifred, dated 7 April 1928, it stated quite simply:

Arthur died yesterday. Winifred.(10)

*A telegram of condolence from Howard Carter. (From the collection of Margaret Orr)*

In a later letter she told Lythgoe how relieved she was that his final illness had lasted only ten days and that he was asleep most of the time. The end, when it came, was in many ways typical of him: he, in Winifred's words '... just lay back, no fuss'. Winifred was there, beside him, as he always wanted her to be, and it was she alone who '... commended his soul to God'.(11)

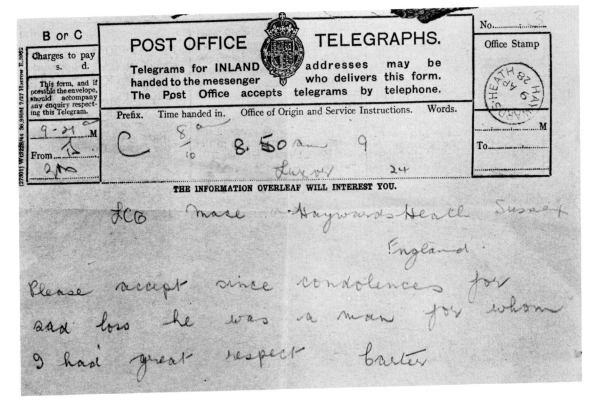

From Britain, America and Egypt came many tributes to his character and his work. The fact that he was an Australian-born Englishman working in Egypt in the service of an American Museum did not go unnoticed at the time and was much admired. His transience might go some way to explain, however, why he has been forgotten. This neglect was not deliberate; he was too highly regarded by his peers for his high standards, hard work and significant contribution to Egyptology. There was admiration and respect from colleagues, his employers and from the Egyptian workmen. On site he was firm yet sympathetic towards his workmen, he spoke their language and came to understand 'the workings of the oriental mind'.(12) There were many personal tributes in letters to Winifred:

It was a privilege to have known your husband and I shall cherish his memory.

Edward A. Harkness

... a fine kindly and splendid man ... so much patient industry and archaeological skill.

Alan H. Gardiner

As you know we not only liked your husband very much personally but also thought very highly of his work ...

Nora Griffith

*The widowed Winifred.*
*(From the collection of*
*Margaret Orr)*

My regard for him was genuine how long I had known him and what respect
I had for his work and abilities.

J. E. Quibell

Lindsley Hall who had so irritated Arthur, wrote a letter of condolence, which indicated that Mace had in fact been very kind to him. Always the diplomat, Arthur had managed to mask his irritation. Hall recalled that once when he was ill, Mace had brought his work into Hall's room so that he might have company. Howard Carter, sent a telegram saying 'He was a man for whom I had great respect'.(13) This was a poor reaction for a man who had played such a significant part in Carter's success. Perhaps there was a follow-up letter, if so it is not extant and perhaps people's responses in the face of death should not be used to judge their character. Nevertheless, in subsequent years Carter did little to make sure his colleague's name was remembered in his own country, let alone make more than a passing reference to the debt he owed him. The Lythgoes were deeply shaken by the loss of their friend; Albert was reported to be visibly distressed.

Inevitably Mace's death, like that of Lord Carnarvon and a number of others, became linked to the so called 'Curse of Tutankhamun'. Ancient Egyptian culture with its cults and mysteries had always been fertile ground for those with spiritual and mystic interests. Symbols derived from Egyptian art and design found their way into Masonic ritual as well as providing backgrounds and story lines for operatic composers. There was a morbid fascination with mummification, which still grips the modern schoolchild and, as Mace himself pointed out, behind much of the general public's interest in archaeology was a Boy's Own mentality about lost treasure. The discovery of the tomb of Tutankhamun was an ideal plot to embroider for one reason or another. The curse seems to have had its origins in an article by the popular novelist Marie Correlli when she wrote that 'the most dire punishment follows any rash intruder into a sealed tomb'.(14) Arthur Conan Doyle, with a noted interest in spiritualism, spoke of the deaths being caused by 'elementals'. There was said to be an inscription in the tomb; 'Death shall come on swift wings to him that toucheth the tomb of the Pharaoh'.(15) In fact no such Hammer House of Horror inscription existed within the tomb which was itself rather short of inscriptions of any sort. Ever plagued by the curse question, the Metropolitan Museum of Art drew up statistics as a standard reply to this rather vexing question.(16) The Metropolitan's statistics revealed that those involved in the excavation of the tomb of Tutankhamun lived well beyond the average age of death for the period. In a sense Tutankhamun did kill Mace, but it was not the curse of the boy King, it was the sheer amount of work involved in clearing the tomb in what were difficult and stressful circumstances. This eventually took its toll on a man who had not been in the best of health since the war, and who since 1897 had lived and worked for much of each year in the heat and dust of the Egyptian desert.

These years had taken their toll on the family as well, particularly on Winifred. There had been twenty-one years of constant travel, separation and concern about money and for nearly ten of these years she had been worried about Arthur's health. At home there was her rather difficult mother and her Downs Syndrome daughter Anne who required constant attention. In addition

there had been her own health and the added worry of Margaret's typhoid which nearly cost the child her life. It was small wonder that photographs of Winifred taken only four years after the winter in the Valley of the Kings show her much aged and careworn. After Arthur's death there were to be few financial worries for her - Lythgoe and Harkness saw to that, but the side of her character that loved life, which delighted in travel, in America, in Egypt and above all 'the river' were, according to her daughter, suppressed and gave way to an over-critical nature which had always simmered beneath the surface. Winifred's love of perfection in all things became more demanding and as perfection is impossible she enjoyed little, whether it was a play or a concert. The years in Egypt, particularly those in which Tutankhamun had played such a large part in her life, were never mentioned, Arthur's papers were put into the attic.(17)

Winifred had her daughters to consider. They moved from Sussex to a house called Shepherds Down in Haslemere, Surrey. Margaret who loved

*Pencil sketch of Winifred Mace.*

*A more relaxed Winifred chats to a friend from the Metropolitan Museum.*

*(From the collection of Margaret Orr)*

Sharrow was not pleased. The move was supposedly for financial reasons, which, as a child, Margaret failed to appreciate particularly as the new house seemed to her, just as large. Children need continuity, Winifred needed change. Before his death Arthur had decided to send Margaret to Benenden School, then a rather new institution with a growing reputation. For Margaret, boarding school was a relief from a home-life that was no longer particularly relaxed or carefree. After school Margaret hoped to follow in her father's footsteps and become an Egyptologist; she was interviewed by Professor Griffith at Oxford who told her archaeology was no career for a woman. In retrospect Margaret believed this was a test and she failed to rise to the bait and left very discouraged by the interview.

Instead her career was to have two strings; one embroidery at the Royal School of Needlework which gave expression to an interest in textiles, inherited from her father; the other was, like her mother, in music and she studied cello and singing. In the 1930s her musical studies took her to Frankfurt where for a time she lived with 'a frightfully Nazi family' who hoped Margaret would marry their son, and she recalls going to hear Adolf Hitler speak at one of the huge pre-war rallies. It was in Haslemere, a country town known for its interest in music that Margaret met and married the brilliant young organ scholar Robin Orr. Together they studied in Paris, Robin specialised in composition and Margaret in singing with Claire Croisa. With the outbreak of the second world war they were back in Britain in a variety of homes. In 1940, Winifred died and Margaret gave birth to twins. As Margaret's life became more and more orientated towards children and her husband's career, inevitably all thoughts of Egypt were pushed to the back of her mind. Margaret's life became that of the wife of a Cambridge don and she came to know many of the outstanding musicians of her generation like Peter Pears and Benjamin Britten. During the war when Robin was 'in intelligence' she had as regular visitors Sarah Churchill and Lady Bonham Carter who from time to time looked after their three children.

Eventually, following Robin's appointment to the new Chair of Music at Glasgow University, the Orrs moved to Kilmacolm and then Lochwinnoch in Renfrewshire. They both quickly became popular and established figures in the west of Scotland and were involved in the embryonic Scottish Opera Company. With them came the collection of Arthur's papers which were once again consigned to the attic of their home. Following their divorce, Margaret remained in Lochwinnoch and for the first time since 1928 had time to look at their family papers. With hopes of publication, Arthur's letters and diaries were typed, but circumstances mitigated against pursuing the project any further and the papers went back into their boxes and the attic. One spring afternoon in 1989 Margaret paid one of her frequent visits to Lochwinnoch's small library housed in the old nineteenth-century village school. Here she spoke to the Curator of the adjoining museum, who, at that time, was researching ancient Egypt for a small exhibition he had promised local schoolchildren. Thinking of her father's papers at home she offered her help; 'Perhaps you might be interested in some things I have at home for your exhibition, you see, my father was an Egyptologist, you won't know of him, Arthur Mace, he's long forgotten'.(18)

*Margaret Orr at her home in Lochwinnoch. (From the collections of the Department of Arts & Libraries, Renfrew District Council. Photograph by Jim Hermit)*

# Postscript

If Mace has been largely forgotten and neglected in Britain then the same cannot be said of his colleagues in New York where his contribution to the growth and development of the Department of Egyptian Art was considerable. Staff at the Metropolitan hold him in high regard as one who helped to establish an early high standard of excavation. In the 1980's the Department went back to excavate at Lisht, working on the south pyramid. They have, since 1991, undertaken field work on the site of Mace's work in and around the north pyramid of Amenemhat I. For this his field note books, over seventy years old, are invaluable. It is a matter of regret to many people that his contribution to the excavations of the tomb of Tutankhamun has received so little acknowledgement; undoubtedly without his conservation skills the excavation and the preservation of objects would not have been nearly so successful. It was also the case that without his diplomatic skills the excavation of the tomb of Tutankhamun might have been an even more acrimonious affair.

Arthur's mother had once expressed her belief that he was especially endowed by gifts from his fairy godmother. These she perceived to have been drawing and poetry. In the light of his contribution to twentieth-century Egyptology many other gifts could be enumerated, but perhaps it was his scholar's love for learning which was most important. In his lecture on Egyptian literature, delivered at the Metropolitan after the war and later printed as a tribute to him, he quoted an ancient Egyptian letter extolling the benefit of learning which was 'a gain for eternity for that which you gain there, is as durable as the hills'.

# References

**(33)** Letter, M. E. Mace to A. C. Mace 11 October 1895.

**(34)** Letter, M. E. Mace to A. C. Mace undated probably 1895.

**(35)** Letter, M. E. Mace to A. C. Mace, 14 July 1896.

## CHAPTER TWO

**(1)** Letter, M. E. Mace to A. C. Mace, 20 November 1892.

**(2)** J. Baines and J. Malek, *Atlas of Ancient Egypt* (1988), 124.

**(3)** M. S. Drower, *Flinders Petrie, A Life in Archaeology* (1985), 193.

**(4)** Drower, 193.

**(5)** P. R. S. Moorey, *Ancient Egypt* (Ashmolean Museum, 1988), 20.

**(6)** Drower, 199.

**(7)** Letter, M. E. Mace to A. C. Mace 20 November 1892.

**(8)** Drower, 232-233.

**(9)** Drower, 232-233. Mrs. Drower originally described Hilda as the model for Aspasia. She has subsequently discovered that this was not the case and that she was in fact the model for the handmaiden. I am grateful to Mrs. Drower for this information.

**(10)** Drower, 244.

**(11)** Egypt Exploration Fund, Memoir XXIII, *Denderah 1898*, W. M. Flinders Petrie, with chapters by F. Ll. Griffith, Dr. Gladstone, and Oldfield Thomas (1900), 1.

**(12)** W. R. Dawson, *Who Was Who in Egyptology* (1951).

**(13)** Dawson and Drower, 246.

**(14)** Drower, 244.

**(15)** H. E. Winlock, *Notes on the Egyptian Expedition*, Metropolitan Museum of Art (1937).

**(16)** Letter, T. E. Lawrence to Mrs. Rieder, 23 January 1912, quoted in M. Brown ed. *The Letters of T. E. Lawrence* (1991)

**(17)** C. Breasted, *The Story of James Henry Breasted Archaeologist* (New York,1948), 75.

**(18)** Breasted, 75.

**(19)** Conversation with Margaret Orr (Mace).

**(20)** Mace journal, Hu, 3 March 1899.

**(21)** Mace journal, Abydos, 30 November 1899.

**(22)** Breasted, 75.

**(23)** Petrie, *Denderah*, 1.

**(24)** Petrie, *Denderah*, 1.

**(25)** Drower, 244.

**(26)** Drower, 247. **(27)** Drower, 247-248.

**(28)** Mace journal, 31 October 1898.

**(29)** Mace journal, 3 November 1898.

**(30)** Mace journal, 7 November 1898.

**(31)** Egypt Exploration Fund Memoir XX, *Diospolis Parva, The Cemeteries of Abadiyeh and Hu*, 1898-99, W. M. Flinders Petrie, with chapters by A. C. Mace (1901).

**(32)** Petrie and Mace, *Diospolis Parva*, 2.

**(33)** Mace journal, Hu, 15 February 1899.

**(34)** Mace journal, Hu, 14 February 1899.

**(35)** Mace journal, Hu, 24 February 1899.

**(36)** Mace journal, Hu, 11 March 1899.

**(37)** Petrie and Mace, *Diospolis Parva*, 53.

**(38)** Mace journal, Hu, 20 February 1899.

**(39)** Mace journal, Hu, 1–2 March 1899.

**(40)** Undated letter from A. C. Mace to M. E. 'Minna' Mace spring 1899.

## CHAPTER ONE

**(1)** Round Robin letters written by Mary Ellen Mace (Minna) between 1889 and 1890. This form of letter writing/journal keeping was very popular in the Mace family (Mace Papers).

**(2)** Arthur's grandfather Bishop Bromby was one of the signatories to a remonstrance addressed by a number of clergy and laity to Mr. T. E. Ellis the Liberal chief whip concerning the party's attitude to The Church.

**(3)** Unattributable journal for November 1865, probably written by a visiting Mace relative from England (Mace Papers). Also notes from Desiree Stephens daughter of Gertrude Mace, Arthur's younger sister.

**(4)** Bishop Bromby's Obituary notice, published by All Souls Church, Clifton.

**(5)** Unattributable newspaper cutting from Tasmania, 1896.

**(6)** Bromby obituary notice.

**(7)** Bromby obituary notice.

**(8)** I am grateful to G. Collins, assistant archivist, Herefordshire and Worcester County Council and Mrs. Paice of Ledbury Library for information about Herefordshire.

**(9)** I am grateful to Anthony Hatfield, Museum Administrator, London Borough of Hackney for this information.

**(10)** Letter, M. A. Bodley to M. E. Mace, Brighton 5 July 1878 (Mace Papers).

**(11)** Letter, undated, Gertrude Mace to A. C. Mace.

**(12)** Round Robin.

**(13)** Conversation with Margaret Orr (nee Mace).

**(14)** Round Robin, 24 December 1889.

**(15)** Round Robin, 4 January 1890.

**(16)** I am grateful for the assistance of B. Allan of the St. Edward's School Archives - Mr. Malcolm, Oxley Deputy Warden of St. Edwards.

**(17)** R. D. Hill; *A History of St. Edward's School* (1962).

**(18)** *A History of St. Edward's School*, 32.

**(19)** *A History of St. Edward's School*, 32.

**(20)** *A History of St. Edward's School*.

**(21)** Round Robin, January 1890.

**(22)** Round Robin, December 1890.

**(23)** Letter, Rev. H. Bromby to A.C. Mace, 26 April 1889 (Mace Papers).

**(24)** Letter, M. E. Mace to A. C. Mace 1891.

**(25)** Round Robin, January 1890.

**(26)** I am grateful to Mike Glasson of the Walsall Leather Centre for much of this information.

**(27)** Obituary of William E. Blyth, *Staffordshire Chronicle*.

**(28)** *Building News*, 18 August 1899.

**(29)** I am grateful to Linda Parry of the Department of Textiles, Victoria and Albert Museum, for this information.

**(30)** Conversation with Mrs Margaret Orr (nee Mace).

**(31)** 'Anyhow' a family magazine produced by the Mace brothers and sisters during school holidays, 1894 (Mace Papers).

**(32)** Round Robin.

(41) Mace journal, Hu, 13 March 1899.

(42) Mace journal, Hu, 17 March 1899.

(43) Mace journal, Hu, 23–24 March 1899.

(44) Egypt Exploration Fund, Memoir XXIII, *El Amrah and Abydos 1899–1901*, D. Randall-MacIver and A. C. Mace (1902).

(45) Mace journal, Abydos, 4 November 1899.

(46) Drower, 256.

(47) Mace journal, Abydos, 11 November 1899.

(48) Mace journal, Abydos, 11 November, 1899. Percy Edward Newberry (1869-1949), Botanist and Egyptologist; Wilhelm Spiegelberg (1870–1930), German Egyptologist. See W. R. Dawson, *Who was Who in Egyptology*.

(49) Mace journal, Abydos, 12 November 1899.

(50) Mace journal, Abydos, 12 November 1899.

(51) Mace journal, Abydos, 14 November 1899.

(52) Mace journal, Abydos, 16 November 1899.

(53) Mace journal, Abydos, 22 November 1899.

(54) Mace journal, Abydos, 28 November 1899.

(55) Mace journal, Abydos, 3 December 1899. The term 'New Race' had been used by Petrie to describe the inhabitants of rather unusual graves first found in 1894-95 at Ballas and Naqada. The graves were so different from those previously found that Petrie put forward the thesis that these were the remains of an invading group. He soon discovered that he was mistaken but not before publishing the excavation report containing his ideas. See T. G. H. James, *Ancient Egypt the Land and the Legacy*, (1988) 171ff.

(56) MacIver and Mace, *El Amrah and Abydos*, 4, and Mace Journal, 28 January 1900.

(57) Mace journal, Abydos, 1 February 1900.

(58) I am indebted to Dr. Dorothea Arnold of the Metropolitan Museum of Art for this information.

(59) Mace journal, Abydos, 3 February 1900.

(60) Mace journal, Abydos, 6 February 1900.

(61) Mace journal, Abydos, 17 February 1900.

(62) Mace journal, Abydos, 9 and 11 February 1900.

(63) Mace journal Abydos, 23 February 1900.

(64) Mace journal, oasis, 7 April 1900.

(65) Mace journal oasis, 11 April 1900.

(66) MacIver and Mace, *El Amrah and Abydos*, 63-66.

(67) Drower, 262.

(68) MacIver and Mace, El Amrah and Abydos, 68.

(69) Mace journal, oasis, 20 April 1900.

(70) Dawson, *Who was Who in Egyptology* (1951), 132.

(71) I am grateful to Mrs. Drower for drawing my attention to these quotations.

(72) Undated letter from M. E. Mace, probably 1902.

(73) Letter, Minna Mace, 1902.

(74) Letter, Minna Mace, 1902.

(75) A. C. Mace; *The Early Dynastic Cemeteries of Naga'ed Dêr* Part II, University of California Publications, Egyptian Archaeology Volume III (Leipzig 1909), VII.

(76) Mace journal, Naga'ed Dêr, 28 November 1901.

(77) Letter, Minna Mace, 1902.

(78) Mace journal, Naga'ed Dêr, 29 November 1901.

(79) Mace journal, Naga'ed Dêr, 29 November 1901.

(80) Mace journal, Naga'ed Dêr, 30 November 1901.

(81) Mace journal, Naga'ed Dêr, 30 November 1901.

(82) Mace journal, Naga'ed Dêr, 22 February 1902.

(83) Mace journal, Giza, 5 May 1903.

(84) Mace, *Early Dynastic Cemeteries*, VII.

(85) G. A. Reisner, *The Excavations of the Hearst Egyptian Expedition of the University of California, 1903-4*. Report to Mrs. Hearst, Phoebe A. Hearst Museum of Anthropology.

(86) Reisner report to Mrs. Hearst, oral report by A. C. Mace.

(87) Reisner report to Mrs. Hearst, oral report by A. C. Mace.

### CHAPTER THREE

(1) *Bulletin of the Metropolitan Museum of Art* (afterwards cited as *B. M. M. A.*) Vol. VI, No.11, New York, November 1911, 203.

(2) H. E. Winlock, *Excavating at Deir el Bahri,* Preface vii and viii M. M. A., New York.

(3) Obituary of A. C. Mace, *Journal of Egyptian Archaeology* Vol., 15 May 1929.

(4) Details of the career of A. C. Mace., M. Hill.

(5) Typescript notes on the Metropolitan Museum of Art Egyptian Expedition, H. E. Winlock, 9 February 1937, supplied by M. Hill.

(6) Details of the career of A. C. Mace, M. Hill.

(7) *B. M. M. A.*, Vol. II No.4, April 1907, 62. This work is based on contemporary preliminary reports. Future publications by Janine Bourriau on the North Pyramid and on the Pyramid and Village by Dieter and Felix Arnold repectively may add clarity to Mace's work.

(8) *B. M. M. A.*, Vol. II No. 10, October 1907 169ff.

(9) Metropolitan Museum of Art, Department of Egyptian Art, Gallery Text, Tomb 763, The North Pyramid Cemetery and A. C. Mace, H. E. Winlock, *The Tomb of Senebtisi at Lisht*, Metropolitan Museum of Art (New York, 1916) Reprint 1973.

(10) *B. M. M. A.*, Vol. II No. 10, October 1907, 169.

(11) *B. M. M. A.*, Vol. II No. 10, October 1907, 169 and Mace and Winlock *Senebtisi* Appendix by Elliot Smith, 119.

(12) Letter, A. C. Mace to Albert M. Lythgoe, 5 January 1908, (Mace File) Metropolitan Museum of Art, New York.

(13) Conversations with Margaret Orr (nee Mace).

(14) Conversations with Marsha Hill, Department of Egyptian Art, M. M. A., New York.

(15) Letter, A. C. Mace to A. M. Lythgoe, 5 January 1908 (Mace File), M. M. A., New York.

(16) *B. M. M. A.*, Vol. III, No. 5, May 1908, 83-84.

(17) *B. M. M. A.*, Vol. III, No. 9, September 1908, 170.

(18) *B. M. M. A.*, Vol. IV, No. 7, July 1909, 119.

(19) Letter, H. E. Winlock to Professor Peet and Obituary.

(20) Letter, H. E. Winlock to Professor Peet and Obituary.

(21) Winlock notes , 9 February 1937.

(22) Letter, H. E. Winlock to Professor Peet and Obituary.

(23) Letter, A. C. Mace to H. E. Winlock, 10 March 1910 (Mace File), M. M. A., New York.

(24) Letter, A. C. Mace to H. E. Winlock, 10 March 1910 (Mace File), M. M. A., New York.

(25) A. C. Mace, *The Murch Collection of Egyptian Antiquities*, *B. M. M. A.*, Vol. VI No 1, January 1911 and W. R. Dawson, *Who was Who in Egyptology* (1951).

(26) A. C. Mace, *The Murch Collection*, 7.

(27) *B. M. M. A.*, Vol. VI, No. 11, November 1911.

(28) Conversation with T. G. H. James C. B. E., Former Keeper

of Egyptian Antiquities with the British Museum.

(29) Letter, A. C. Mace to C. Ransom, February 1913 (Mace file), M. M. A., New York.

(30) *B. M. M. A.*, Vol. IX, No. 10, October 1914, 203ff.

(31) *B. M. M. A.*, Vol. IX, No. 10, October 1910, 214.

(32) Letter, A. C. Mace to A. M. Lythgoe, 12 August 1914 (Mace File), M. M. A., New York.

(33) Letter, A. M. Lythgoe to A. C. Mace, 25 September 1914 (Mace file), M. M. A., New York.

(34) Letter, A. C. Mace to A. M. Lythgoe, 12 August 1914 (Mace File), M. M. A., New York.

(35) Letter, A. C. Mace to A. M. Lythgoe, 3 September 1914 (Mace File), M. M. A., New York.

(36) Letter, A. C. Mace to A. M. Lythgoe, 2 September 1914 (Mace File), M. M. A., New York.

(37) Letter, A. C. Mace to H. E. Winlock, 15 April 1915 (Mace File), M. M. A., New York.

(38) Letter, A. C. Mace to H. E. Winlock, 9 February 1915 (Mace File), M. M. A., New York.

(39) Letter, H. E. Winlock to A. C. Mace, 22 March 1915 (Mace File), M. M. A., New York.

(40) Letter, A. C. Mace to A. M. Lythgoe, 27 August 1915 (Mace File), M. M. A., New York.

(41) Letter, A. C. Mace to A. M. Lythgoe, 15 September 1915 (Mace File), M. M. A., New York.

(42) Letter, A. C. Mace to A. M. Lythgoe, 27 August 1915 (Mace File), M. M. A., New York.

(43) Letter, A. C. Mace, to A. M. Lythgoe, 26 June 1916 (Mace File), M. M. A., New York.

(44) Postcard to the Metropolitan Museum of Art, 25 February 1919 (Mace File), M. M. A., New York.

(45) Letter to A. C. Mace to A. M. Lythgoe, 22 March 1917 (Mace File), M. M. A., New York.

(46) *B. M. M. A.*, Vol. XII, No. 3, March 1917, 73.

(47) *B. M. M. A.*, Vol. XII, October 1917. For a more recent summary of the situation see J. Bourriau, *Pharaohs and Mortals*, Cambridge 1988, 85–87.

(48) Letter, A. M. Lythgoe to A. C. Mace, 16 May 1918 (Mace File), M. M. A., New York.

(49) Letters A. C. Mace to A. M. Lythgoe, 1 January 1919 and 2 February 1919 (Mace File), M. M. A., New York.

(50) Letter, A. M. Lythgoe to A. C. Mace, 13 January 1919 (Mace File), M. M. A., New York.

(51) A. C. Mace, *The Caskets of the Princess Sit-hathor-yunet. B. M. M. A.*, Vol. XV, No. 7, July 1920, 151-156.

(52) Letter, A. M. Lythgoe to A. C. Mace, 3 September 1920, (Mace File) M. M. A., New York.

(53) A. M. Lythgoe's preface to *Egyptian Literature*; A Lecture by Arthur Cruttenden Mace, published in memoriam by the Metropolitan Museum of Art in 1928.

(54) A. C. Mace *Egyptian Literature*, 15-16. Thus in the Hymn to Aton:

> How manifold thy world, beyond our knowledge,
> O God, there is none other like to thee.
> Thou, and thou only, didst create the heavens,
> The earth beneath, and all that moves therein -
> Men, cattle great and small, that walk upon their feet,
> All creatures of the air, that fly upon their wings.

And in Psalm 104:

> Thou makest darkness and it is night:
> Wherein all the beasts of the forest creep forth.
> The young lions war after their prey.
> Man goeth forth to his work, and to his labour until the evening.
> There go the ships and there is that Leviathan
> How manifold are thy works...

(55) Letter, A. C. Mace to Winifred Mace, 27 November 1920.

(56) Letter, A. C. Mace to Winifred Mace, 28 November 1920.

(57) Letter, A. C. Mace to A. M. Lythgoe, 29 December 1920 (Mace File), M. M. A., New York.

(58) A. M. Lythgoe, *The Egyptian Expedition 1920-1921, B. M. M. A.*, November 1921.

(59) Letter, A. C. Mace to Winifred Mace, 21 February 1921.

(60) Letter, A. C. Mace to Winifred Mace, 23 February 1921.

(61) Letter, A. C. Mace to Winifred Mace, 12 January 1921.

(62) Letter, A. C. Mace to A. M. Lythgoe, 6 December 1921 (Mace File), M. M. A., New York.

(63) Letter, A. M. Lythgoe to A. C. Mace, 7 February 1922 (Mace File), M. M. A., New York.

(64) Letter, A. C. Mace to A. M. Lythgoe, 13 February 1922 (Mace File), M. M. A., New York.

(65) Letter, A. C. Mace to Winifred Mace, 7 February 1922.

(66) Letter, A. M. Lythgoe to A. C. Mace, 17 November 1922 (Mace File), M. M. A., New York.

(67) Letter, A. M. Lythgoe to A. C. Mace, 17 November 1922 (Mace File), M. M. A., New York.

(68) A. C. Mace, The Excavations at Lisht, *B. M. M. A.*, December 1922 and Letter from A. C. Mace to Winifred Mace, 18 February 1922.

## CHAPTER FOUR

(1) N. Reeves, *The Complete Tutankhamun* (1990), 56.

(2) See: N. Reeves, *The Complete Tutankhamun*; T G. H. James, *Howard Carter, The Trail to Tutankhamun* (1992); H. V. F. Winstone, *Howard Carter and the Discovery of the tomb of Tutankhamun* (1991); Christiane Desroches-Noblecourt, *Tutankhamun, Life and Death of a Pharaoh* (1972). For a more controversial study see T. Hoving, *Tutankhamun, the Untold Story* (1979) and of course the first hand account itself, H. Carter and A. C. Mace, *The Tomb of Tutankhamun* (various editions).

(3) Howard Carter to Lord Carnarvon, quoted N. Reeves, 50.

(4) Quoted in N. Reeves, 54.

(5) A. C. Mace, *Work at the Tomb of Tutankhamun, the Egyptian Expedition, B. M. M. A.* (part II) December 1923.

(6) *Wonderful Things*, M. M. A., New York, 1976, xiv.

(7) Henry (Harry) Burton, 1879-1940, born Lincolnshire and lived in Florence.

(8) *Wonderful Things*, M. M. A., xv.

(9) Quotation from notes kindly made available by Marsha Hill on the career of A. C. Mace in the Department of Egyptian Art, M. M. A., New York.

(10) Quoted by T. G. H. James in Howard Carter, *The Trail to Tutankhamun* (1992). I am extremely grateful to Mr. James for allowing me to see the relevant Mace sections of his biography of Carter, prior to publication.

(11) *B. M. M. A.*, *The Egyptian Expedition, 3*, December 1923.
(12) *B. M. M. A.*, *The Egyptian Expedition, 3*, December 1923.
(13) Conversation with M. Hill, M. M. A..
(14) Letter, A. C. Mace to Winifred Mace, 26 December 1922.
(15) *Wonderful Things*, M. M. A., xi.
(16) Letter, A. C. Mace to Winifred Mace, 12 February 1923 and *Wonderful Things*, M. M. A., xiii.
(17) Letter, A. C. Mace to Winifred Mace, 26 December 1922.
(18) Letter, A. C. Mace to Winifred Mace, 26 December 1922.
(19) Letter, A. C. Mace to Winifred Mace, 29 December 1922.
(20) Carter and Mace, 106.
(21) Letter, A. C. Mace to Winifred Mace, 28 December 1922 and Hoving 116.
(22) Carter and Mace, 106-107.
(23) Letter, A. C. Mace, to Winifred Mace, 6 January 1923.
(24) Carter and Mace, 110.
(25) Letter, A. C. Mace to Winifred Mace, 21 January 1923.
(26) Letter A. C. Mace to Winifred Mace, 6 February 1923.
(27) Letter, A. C. Mace to Winifred Mace, 6 February 1923.
(28) A. C. Mace field diary, 27 December 1922 to 13 May 1923, entry for 5 February 1923. Diary on loan to the Griffith Institute, Oxford.
(29) Carter and Mace, 111-112.
(30) Letter, A. C. Mace, to Winifred Mace, 9 February 1923.
(31) *B. M. M. A.*, December 1923.
(32) Letter, A. M. Lythgoe to Edward Robinson, quoted in *Wonderful Things*, M. M. A., New York, 1976.
(33) Letter, A. C. Mace, to Winifred Mace, 18 February 1923.
(34) Letters, A. C. Mace to Winifred Mace, 7 February and 7 March 1923.
(35) Letter, A. C. Mace to Winifred Mace, 4 January 1923.
(36) Letter, A. C. Mace to Winifred Mace, 9 January 1923.
(37) Letter, A. C. Mace to Winifred Mace, 29 March 1923.
(38) Letter, A. C. Mace to Winifred Mace, 7 January 1923.
(39) Letter, A. C. Mace to Winifred Mace, 7 February 1923.
(40) Letter, A. C. Mace to Winifred Mace, 8 January 1923.
(41) Letter, A. C. Mace to Winifred Mace, 21 January 1923.
(42) Letter, A. C. Mace to Winifred Mace, 17 April 1923.
(43) Letter, A. C. Mace to Mrs. Blyth, 16 April 1923.
(44) H. V. F. Winstone, *Howard Carter*, 227ff.
(45) Letter, A. C. Mace to Winifred Mace, 24 April 1923.
(46) *The Times* 23 January 1923.
(47) *The Times*.
(48) Letter, A. C. Mace to Winifred Mace, 9 January 1923.
(49) Letter, A. C. Mace to Winifred Mace, 21 January 1923.
(50) Letter, A. C. Mace to Winifred Mace, 26 January 1923.
(51) Letter, A. C. Mace to Winifred Mace, 26 January 1923.
(52) H. V. F. Winstone, *Howard Carter*, 174.
(53) H. V. F. Winstone, *Howard Carter*, 262 and conversation with Mrs. Margaret Orr (Mace).
(54) Letter, A. C. Mace to Winifred Mace, 26 January, 1923.
(55) Letter, A. C. Mace to Winifred Mace, 23 and 28 January 1923.
(56) Letter, A. C. Mace to Winifred Mace, 28 January and 7 February 1923.
(57) Letter, A. C. Mace to Winifred Mace, 9 February 1923.
(58) N. Reeves, *Complete Tutankhamun*, 64.
(59) Conversation with Margaret Orr.
(60) Letter, A. C. Mace to Winifred Mace, 28 April 1923.
(61) Letter, A. C. Mace to Winifred Mace, 12 February and 13 January, 1923.
(62) Letter, A. C. Mace to Winifred Mace, 14 February 1923.
(63) Letter, A. C. Mace to Winifred Mace, 18 February 1923.
(64) Letter, A. C. Mace to Winifred Mace, 10 March 1923.
(65) 'Letters from cranks'.
(66) Letter, A. C. Mace to Winifred Mace, 15 February 1923.
(67) A. C. Mace, field diary, 1922-1923 Griffith Institute, Oxford.
(68) Letter, A. C. Mace to Winifred Mace, 17 February 1923.
(69) Letter, A. C. Mace to Winifred Mace, 17 February 1923, and a description written by Mace at the Cataract Hotel, Aswan on 3 March 1923.
(70) Letter, A. C. Mace to Winifred Mace, 28 February 1923.
(71) Highclere Castle, Lord Carnarvon's home near Newbury, Berkshire. Letter, A. C. Mace to Winifred Mace, 3 March 1923.
(72) Letter, A. C. Mace to Winifred Mace 19 March 1923.
(73) Letter, A. C. Mace to Mrs. Blyth, 11 April 1923.
(74) Letter, A. C. Mace to Winifred Mace, 17 April 1923.

## CHAPTER FIVE

(1) Letter, A. C. Mace to A. M. Lythgoe, 18 October 1923 (Mace File), M. M. A., New York.
(2) Undated letter, December 1923.
(3) Letter, 15 December 1923.
(4) Letter, 15 December 1923.
(5) Letter, 21 December 1923.
(6) Letter, 21 December 1923.
(7) Letter, 21 December 1923.
(8) Letter, 21 December 1923.
(9) Letter, 21 December 1923.
(10) Letter, 21 December 1923.
(11) Letter, 21 December 1923.
(12) *The New York Times*, 30 and 31 January, 7 February 1940.
(13) Letter, 23 December 1923.
(14) Letter, 23 December 1923.
(15) Letter, 23 December 1923.
(16) Letter, 23 December 1923.
(17) Conversation with Margaret Orr. (18) Letter, 23 December 1923.
(19) Hon. Richard Bethell, son of 3rd Baron Westbury.
(20) A form of charades - letter, 23 December 1923.
(21) Letter, 16 January 1924.
(22) Letter, 1 January 1924.
(23) Conversation with Margaret Orr.
(24) Letter, 21 January 1924.
(25) Letter, 16 January 1924.
(26) Letter, 20 January 1924. Sir Robert Ludwig Mond (1867-1938), chemist and archaeologist.
(27) W. R. Dawson, *Who was who in Egyptology* (1951), 110.
(28) Letter, 20 January 1924.
(29) Letters, 3 and 13 February 1924.
(30) Letter, 21 January 1924. Nina de Garis Davies made coloured reproductions of selected scenes in Egyptian tombs. Her husband Norman (1865-1941) was the foremost of the copyists.
(31) Letter, 23 January 1924.

(32) Letter, 23 January 1924 and conversation with Margaret Orr.
(33) Letter, 20 January 1924 and conversation with Margaret Orr.
(34) Letter, 16 January 1924.
(35) Letter, 16 January 1924.
(36) Conversation with Margaret Orr.
(37) Letter, 13 January 1924.
(38) Marsha Hill, The Career of Henry Burton, in Erik Horning, *The Tomb of Pharaoh Seti I, Zurich*, 1991.
(39) Letters, 13 and 31 January 1924.
(40) Letters, 16, 20, 31 January 17, 24 February, 1924.
(41) Letter, 16 January 1924.
(42) Letter, 31 January 1924.
(43) Letter, 31 January 1924.
(44) Letter, 10 February 1924.
(45) Letter, 13 February 1924.
(46) Letter, 13 February 1924.
(47) Letter, 13 February 1924 and Letter, A. M. Lythgoe to A. C. Mace, 30 May, 1924, (Mace File) M. M. A., New York.
(48) Letter, 14 February 1924.
(49) Letter, 24 February 1924.
(50) Letter, 24 February 1924.
(51) Letter, 12 March 1924.
(52) Letter, 14 March 1924.
(53) Letter, W. Mace to A. Blyth 15 April 1924 and A. C. Mace to Mrs. Blyth 14 April 1924.

## CHAPTER SIX

(1) Letter, Winifred Mace to Mrs. Blyth, 20 March 1924.
(2) Letter, A. C. Mace, to A. M. Lythgoe, July 1926 (Mace File), M. M. A., New York.
(3) Letter, A. C. Mace, to A. M. Lythgoe, 14 January 1927 (Mace File), M. M. A., New York.
(4) S. Alstead, J. Gordon MacArthur, eds. *Clinical Pharmacology,* (1965)
(5) Letter, A. C. Mace to A. M. Lythgoe, 14 January 1927 (Mace File), M. M. A., New York.
(6) Letter, A. C. Mace to A. M. Lythgoe, 7 August 1927 (Mace File), M. M. A., New York.
(7) Letter, A. C. Mace to A. M. Lythgoe, 7 August 1927 (Mace File), M. M. A., New York.
(8) Letter, Winifred Mace to Edward Harkness, 7 October 1927 (Mace File), M. M. A., New York.
(9) Letter, A.C. Mace to Lucy Lythgoe, 14 March 1928 (Mace File), M. M. A., New York.
(10) Telegram, Winifred Mace to A. M. Lythgoe, 7 April 1928 (Mace File), M. M. A., New York.
(11) Letter, Winifred Mace to A. M. Lythgoe, 18 April 1928 (Mace File), M. M. A., New York.
(12) A. C. Mace Obituary, *Journal of Egyptian Archaeology*, Vol. X, May 1929.
(13) Telegram, Howard Carter to Winifred Mace, 28 April 1928
(14) Quoted, N. Reeves, Complete Tutankhamun, 62
(15) Quoted N. Reeves, Complete Tutankhamun, 63
(16) The Curse of the Pharaohs; A Brief Assessment. M. M. A., New York, 1978. I am grateful to Marsha Hill for drawing this to my attention.
(17) Conversation with Margaret Orr (Mace).
(18) I am grateful to Mrs. Margaret Orr for the many hours of her time she gave up to talk to me about her father.

# Bibliography and Sources

## 1. PRIMARY SOURCES

**(i) The Papers of Arthur C. Mace**

'Round Robin', a series of letters written in journal form for the benefit of family and friends by Mary Ellen Mace, 1889–1890; unattributable journal written in Tasmania in 1864 probably by a visiting Mace relative from England; a collection of letters to Arthur Mace from members of his family including: the Rev. John Mace, M. E. Mace, Hilda Mace, Gertrude Mace, M. A. Bodley and the Rev. Henry Bromby; 'Anyhow', the Mace family magazine produced by Arthur and his brothers and sisters.

**Journals and letters written by Mace in Egypt**

Journal at Hu 1898–1899; journal written at Abydos 1899–1901; journal written while on a visit to the Kharga Oasis 1900; journal written at Naga'ed Dêr 1901; journal written at Giza 1903. A collection of letters written by Arthur to his wife Winifred from Lisht and subsequently Thebes 1920-1923. A collection of letters written to Howard Carter or Lord Carnarvon from eccentrics, kept by Mace and labelled 'Letters from Cranks'. A collection of letters written by Winifred Mace to her mother Mrs. Blyth from the Metropolitan House in Thebes 1923–1924. A collection of telegrams and letters of condolence written to Winifred Mace following Arthur's death in 1928.

**(ii) Metropolitan Museum of Art New York, Department of Egyptian Art**

A. C. Mace files. These files contain correspondence between A. C. Mace and A. M. Lythgoe from the early days of the department until Mace's death. There is also some correspondence between Mace and H. E. Winlock.

**(iii) Griffith Institute, Ashmolean Museum Oxford**

The Field Diary of A. C. Mace 27 December 1922 to 13 May 1923.

**(iv) Phoebe A. Hearst Museum of Anthropology, University of California at Berkeley**

The Excavations of the Hearst Egyptian Exhibition of the University of California, 1903-1904. Report by G. A. Reisner (with contribution by Mace) to Mrs. Hearst.

## 2. OTHER PRINTED SOURCES AND ARCHIVES

Obituary notice for Bishop Bromby, All Souls, Clifton, England. Metropolitan Museum of Art, New York, Gallery Text Department of Egyptian Art; M. M. A., *The Curse of the Pharaohs, a Brief Assessment* (1978); Marsha Hill, Various notes on the career of A. C. Mace also: Winlock, H. E., Notes on the Egyptian Expedition M. M. A., 1937; Winlock, H. E., Excavating at Deir el Bahri. M. M. A.

## 3. ORAL SOURCES

Conversations with: Margaret Orr; Marsha Hill; Dorothea and Dieter Arnold; Harry James, Nicholas Reeves; Malcolm Oxley; Jaromir Malek.

## 4. NEWSPAPERS AND PERIODICALS

*The Times*; *The New York Times*; *Staffordshire Chronicle*; *Oxford Guardian*; *Building News*; *The Mercury* (Hobart Tasmania); *The Illustrated London News*.

## SECONDARY SOURCES

**(i) Journals**

*Bulletin of the Metropolitan Museum of Art (B.M.M.A.)*; *Journal of Egyptian Archaeology*.

**(ii) Other Secondary Sources**

(Place of Publication London unless otherwise stated.) Alstead, S. and MacArthur, J. Gordon, *Clinical Pharmacology* (1965); Baines J. and Malek J., *Atlas of Ancient Egypt* (1988); Breasted, C.,*The Story of James Henry Breasted, Archaeologist* (New York, 1948); Carter, H., and Mace, A. C., *The Tomb of Tutankhamun* (1923); Dawson, W. R., *Who was Who in Egyptology* (1951); Dorman, P. F., Oliver Harper, P. and Pittman, H., *The Metropolitan Museum of Art, Egypt and the Near East* (New York, 1987); Drower, M. S., Flinders Petrie, *A Life in Archaeology* (1985); Hayes, W. C., *The Sceptre of Egypt, A Background for the Study of the Egyptian Antiquities in the Metropolitan Museum of Art* (New York, 1953); Hill, R. D., *A History of St. Edward's School* (1962); Horning, E., *The Tomb of Pharaoh Seti I* (Zurich, 1991); Hoving, T., *Tutankhamun, The Untold Story* (1979); James, T. G. H., *Ancient Egypt The Land and the Legacy* (1988); James, T. G. H., *Howard Carter, the Trail to Tutankhamun* (1992); Mace, A. C., *The Early Dynastic Cemeteries of Naga'ed Dêr Part II;* University of California Publications, *Egyptian Archaeology Vol. III,* (Leipzig 1909) *Vol. VII*; Mace, A. C., and Winlock, H. E., *The Tomb of Senebtisi at Lisht* (New York, 1916 reprint 1973); Mace A. C., *Egyptian Literature.* A lecture by Arthur Cruttenden Mace, published in memorium (New York, 1928); Merrilees, R. S., *Living with Egypt's Past in Australia* (Museum of Victoria, Melbourne, 1990); Metropolitan Museum of Art, *Wonderful Things* (New York, 1976); Moorey, P. R. S., *Ancient Egypt* (Ashmolean Museum 1988); Noblecourt, Christiane Desroches, *Tutankhamun Life and Death of a Pharaoh* (1972); Petrie, W. M. Flinders, Egypt Exploration Fund Memoir XXIII *Denderah 1898* with chapters by F. Ll. Griffith, Dr. Gladstone and Oldfield Thomas (1900); Petrie, W. M. Flinders, Egypt Exploration Fund, Memoir XX, *Diospolis Parva, the Cemeteries of Abadiyeh and Hu 1898-1899* with chapters by A. C. Mace (1901); Randall-MacIver, D. and Mace, A. C., Egypt Exploration Fund, Memoir XXIII, *El Amrah and Abydos 1899-1901* (1902); Reeves, N., *The Complete Tutankhamun* (1990); Sattin, Anthony, *Lifting the Veil, British Society in Egypt 1768-1956* (1988); Stephens, The Reverend Dr. Canon Geoffrey, *The Anglican Church in Tasmania, A Diocesan History to Mark the Sesqui-Centenary* (Hobart, 1969); Winstone, H. V. F., *Howard Carter and the Discovery of The Tomb of Tutankhamun* (1991)

# Index

Abadiyeh, excavation at, 39
Abydos, excavations at, 43-49 *passim*
Akhenaten, Pharaoh, 32, 76
Amarna, excavation at, 31-33
Amenemhat I, King,
    pyramid and cemetery of, 58, 59, 63, 78, 149
El Amrah, 46, 49
Arab workmen, Mace's relationship with, 46-47, 64
'Artists Rifles', 70
Ashmolean Museum, Oxford, 32, 38
Aswan, visit by Mace to, 109

Bethell, Richard, 104, 119, 129
Blyth, Adie ('Granny Blyth'), 25, 27, 61, 93
Blyth, William E., 25, 27, 53, 61
Blyth, Winifred, see Mace, Winifred
Bromby, Charles Henry, Bishop of Tasmania, 17, 18
Bromby, Mary Ellen (Minna), see Mace, Mary Ellen
Burton, Henry (Harry), 82-83, 104, 117
Burton, Minnie, 117, 130, 134

Cairo Museum, 41, 83, 115
Callender, Arthur R. ('Pecky'), 94, 104
Carnarvon, Lord (George Herbert, 5th Earl of Carnarvon):
    patron of Howard Carter, 81, 82; involvement in
    Tutankhamun excavation, 83, 95, 101, 104, 109;
    arrangement with *The Times*, 99; letters to, from
    'cranks', 101-102; death of, 110-111, 143
Carter, Howard, 44, 81-111 *passim*, 120, 129, 138, 143;
    discovery of the tomb of Tutankhamun, 81-82; accepts
    assistance of Metropolitan Museum, 82-83; Mace's
    relationship with, 85-86, 94-96; opening of the burial
    chamber, 103-104, 107; difficulties with the Egyptian
    authorities, 115, 119, 126, 132-134; Winifred Mace's
    opinion of, 130, 132

Davies, Norman de Garis, 34, 47, 64
Denderah, excavation at, 33, 34, 37, 38
Diospolis Parva, see Hu

Egyptology, Mace's contribution to, 149

Gardiner, Alan, 104, 115, 119, 133, 142
Giza, Pyramids of, excavations at, 53, 54

Hall, Lindsley, 68, 76, 84-85, 92, 94, 143

Harkness, Edward, 117, 119, 137, 138, 142
Harkness, Mary, 120, 130
Hathor, Egyptian goddess, temple of, 37
Hauser, Walter, 83, 94, 111, 117
Hearst, Phoebe, 51
Herbert, Lady Evelyn, 82, 104, 109
Herbert, George, 5th Earl of Carnarvon, see Carnarvon, Lord
Hu (Huw or Hiu), 36, 38; excavations at, 39-43

Italy, visits by Mace to, 38-39, 134-135

Jones, W. J., 64

Keble College, Oxford, 28
Kharga Oasis, visit of Mace to, 47, 49; excavations at, 62-64
Kuanaten, see Akhenaten, Pharaoh

Lacau, Pierre, 104, 115, 133, 134
El Lahun, pyramid and cemetery at, 73
Lahun jewel caskets, Mace's reconstruction of, 73, 75
Lansing, Ambrose, 66-67, 79
Lawes, Miss, 39, 45, 46
Lawrence, T. E., 35
Lisht, Pyramids of, excavations at, 58-61, 63-64, 66, 67,
    76-78, 79, 149
Lochwinnoch (Scotland), 146
Lucas, Alfred, 84, 87, 88, 104, 119-120
Luxor, 42, 115, 123-124, 133
Lythgoe, Albert Morton: excavations with Mace at Naga'ed
    Dêr, 51, 54; first Curator of Egyptian Art at Metropolitan
    Museum, 58-79 *passim*; involves Museum in Tutankhamun
    excavation, 82-83; his involvement in the Tutankhamun
    excavation, 92, 104, 117, 130, 138
Lythgoe, Lucy, 59, 119, 120, 124, 130

Mace, Arthur Cruttenden: birth and early childhood in
    Tasmania, 16-18, 78; family background, 17-20, 29;
    childhood and home life in England, 20-21; schooling,
    21-23; hobbies, 27-28; university, 28; 'apprenticeship' with
    Flinders Petrie, 33-49 *passim*; assistant to George Reisner,
    49-55; appointment to staff of Metropolitan Museum of
    Art, New York, 57; marriage, 61; war service, 69-71, 73;
    his contributions to the Tutankhamun excavation, 86-88,
    91-92, 95, 103-104, 111, 119-120, 132-134; ill-health, 66,
    70, 73, 76, 134-140 *passim*; after Tutankhamun, 137-141;
    death, 141, 143; tributes to, 142-143
Mace, Henry ('Uncle Henry'), 21, 23
Mace, Reverend John (father), 16, 17, 18, 19
Mace, Mary Ellen (Minna) (mother), 17, 18-20
Mace, Winifred (wife), 25, 61-62, 73, 93, 140-141, 143-144;
    Mace's letters to, 76-110 *passim*; visit to Egypt with
    Margaret, 114-134 *passim*; visit to tomb of Tutankhamun,
    119-120; her attitude to Egypt and Egyptians, 125-126; her

opinion of Mace's colleagues, 130, 132
Mace, Margaret Ellen (daughter), 67, 78, 92-93, 113-114,
    145-146; visit to Egypt with Winifred, 114-134 *passim*;
    ·visit to tomb of Tutankhamun, 119-120
Mace, Anne (daughter), 73, 93, 113
MacIver, David Randall, 34, 42, 43, 46, 47, 49, 50
Maspero, Gaston, 44, 59
Metropolitan House, Egypt, 84, 117-134 *passim*
Metropolitan Museum of Art, New York: establishment of
    Department of Egyptian Art, 55, 57; appointment of
    Lythgoe, Mace and Winlock to staff, 57; appointment of
    Mace as Assistant Curator of Egyptian Art, 64-65; Mace's
    work on the Murch Collection, 65-66; publications by
    Mace, 66, 72; Mace's restoration of the Lahun caskets,
    73, 75; Mace's lecture on Egyptian literature, 75-76;
    becomes involved in the Tutankhamun excavation, 82-83;
    statistics regarding the curse of Tutankhamun, 143

Mond, Robert, 124-125
Morgan, J. Pierpont, 64, 68, 84
Murch Collection of Egyptian antiquities,
    Mace's work on, 65-66

Naga'ed Dêr, visit of Mace to, 50; excavations at, 51-54
Nectanebo, King, temple of, at Kharga, 49
Neferneferuaten-Tasherit, Princess, 32
Neferneferure, Princess, 32
Nefertiti, Queen, 32
Newberry, Percy, 44, 115, 119

Orme, Beatrice, 39, 46
Orr, Margaret, see Mace, Margaret Ellen
Orr, Robin, 146
Oxford Movement, 15, 21

Petrie, Hilda, 32, 42-43
Petrie, William Matthew Flinders, 31-55 *passim*, 58, 65,
    66, 73; Mace's 'apprenticeship' with, 33-49 *passim*
Pharaoh, Miss Lillian, 101
Photography, 51-53

Quibell, James, 44, 143

Reisner, George Andrew, 49, 50, 51, 53; Mace's work as
    assistant to, 49-55
Robinson, Edward, 78, 83

St. Edward's School, Oxford, 21-23
Sit-hathor-yunet, Princess, grave of, 73
Senebtisi, tomb of, 59-61, 66, 72-73
Senwosret I, King, pyramid of, 58-59

Senwosret II, King, pyramid and cemetery of, 73
Seti II, King, tomb of, 87
Sewadjenra, King, dagger of, 41
Smith, G. Elliot, 61

Tasmania, 16, 17, 18, 78
Thebes, visit by Mace to, 44; excavation at, 83
*The Times*, Mace's articles in, 96, 99; Carnarvon's
    arrangement with, 99
*The Tomb of Senebtisi at Lisht*, by Mace and Winlock, 72-73
*The Tomb of Tutankhamun*, by Mace and Carter, 132
Tutankhamun, Curse of, 15, 99, 143
Tutankhamun excavation: first season, 81-111; discovery of
    the tomb, 80-81; Mace's role, 81, 86-91; Mace's
    relationship with Howard Carter, 85-86, 94-96; difficulties
    with the press, 99-100; visitors to, 100-101; 'letters from
    cranks', 101, 103; opening of the burial chamber, 103-104,
    107; second season, 113-135; difficulties with the Egyptian
    authorities, 115, 119, 126, 130, 132-134; life at
    Metropolitan House, 117-134 *passim*; visitors, 124-125;
    work on the tomb, 132-133

Unwin, F. L., 64
Urlin, Hilda, see Petrie, Hilda

Valley of the Kings, 81, 94, 103, 119

Weigall, Arthur, 99, 135
Winter Palace Hotel, Luxor, 115, 120, 124
Wilkin, Anthony, 45, 47, 49
Winlock, Frances, 117, 124, 127, 129
Winlock, Helen, 84, 93, 123, 130
Winlock, Herbert Eustis, 64, 65, 72-73, 79, 84, 104, 109, 132;
    joins staff of Metropolitan Museum, 57; excavations with
    Mace at Lisht, 58-61, 63; Mace's relationship with, 68-69,
    76, 92-93, 130